Penguin Books
Feeding Your Family

Miriam Stoppard, MD, MRCP, practised clinical medicine for seven years, specializing in dermatology for the last three, before joining a major drug company working in clinical research. She was Medical Director, then Managing Director before leaving in 1980 to devote herself full-time to writing, broadcasting and medical education.

Miriam Stoppard was Radio London's resident phone-in doctor from 1970 to 1972 and presented the BBC radio series *Well Woman*, devoted to problems of women's health. Dr Stoppard was medical presenter on television's *Don't Ask Me, Don't Just Sit There, The Health Show, So You Want to Stop Smoking, Where There's Life* and *Baby & Co.* She has contributed articles to many leading magazines, and writes a syndicated newspaper column on medical matters. Her books include *Miriam Stoppard's Book of Health Care*, the best-selling *Every Woman's Lifeguide, Your Baby, Your Growing Child, The Pregnancy and Birth Book, The Prime of Your Life* and *Every Girl's Lifeguide*.

Miriam Stoppard is married to the playwright Tom Stoppard and has two sons and two stepsons.

Feeding Your Family

Miriam Stoppard

PENGUIN BOOKS

PENGUIN BOOKS

Published by the Penguin Group
27 Wrights Lane, London W8 5TZ (Publishing and Editorial)
and Harmondsworth, Middlesex, England (Distribution and Warehouse)
Viking Penguin Inc., 40 West 23rd Street, New York, New York 10010, USA
Penguin Books Australia Ltd, Ringwood, Victoria, Australia
Penguin Books Canada Ltd, 2801 John Street, Markham, Ontario, Canada L3R 1B4
Penguin Books (NZ) Ltd, 182–190 Wairau Road, Auckland 10, New Zealand

Penguin Books Ltd. Registered Office: Harmondsworth, Middlesex, England

First published by Viking 1987
Published in Penguin Books 1988

Made and printed in Great Britain by
Richard Clay (The Chaucer Press) Ltd, Bungay, Suffolk
Filmset in Linotron Trump Medieval

Photographic Acknowledgements
The photographs in this Book were taken by: Nancy Durrell-McKenna, 2, 128;
Andra Nelki, 6, 12, 44, 68, 88, 176; Jason Shenai, 144, 192.

The photographs in this Book were taken by: Nancy Durrell-McKenna, 128;
Andra Nelki, 6, 12, 44, 68, 88, 176; Jason Shenai, 144, 192.

Contents

Introduction

There are so many controversies in the field of nutrition that it's impossible for a book of this kind to satisfy everyone. Some readers will find that it doesn't go far enough and that some of the advice I give is too soft. Other people, probably many more, will feel that the book goes too far, that it's unrealistic because they think the advice I give is too difficult for them to put into practice. I feel, therefore, that it is important for me to tell you what my position is.

My aim is to make it easy for people to change from an unhealthy way of eating to a healthier one. I am not insisting on very great changes. That kind of tough line has failed and always will because it is impossible to maintain sweeping changes in eating habits for more than a few months. Research has shown that simply cutting down, or eliminating, our consumption of certain foods can make a great difference to our health in a short time. To help people achieve this goal I suggest changes that may take some effort, but really do not impose any hardship. I would much rather help a large number of people to incorporate small changes into their eating habits for life than help a few people make very great changes, probably only temporarily.

I subscribe to the old 80/20 rule: as long as you eat the right foods 80 per cent of the time, it hardly matters what you eat the other 20 per cent. Many purists will be shocked, but I stick to this rule because, firstly, I think it's accurate and true, and, secondly, it encourages compliance.

Contrary to popular belief, a healthy diet is not the same as a permanent calorie-counting one. The healthiest diet for human beings is one drawn from the greatest variety of sources. There are some foods that, partly because of advertising and partly because of the mass media, we have come to think of as 'naughty'. But foods such as fish and chips, hamburgers, pizza, fried eggs and bacon, and even cake are naughty only to purists. I see them as a part, albeit a very small one, of a normal diet. While I would not suggest people indulge in them frequently, normally there is no harm in having them occasionally.

Another popular misconception is that foods described as 'low-calorie' are synonymous with slimming. In this book low-calorie foods are not intended as slimming foods. For example, I advocate low-calorie snack foods because everybody should be able to have a snack now and then without adding greatly to the daily calorie intake, which could lead to a gain in weight.

Some people also think that it is impossible to prevent youngsters from eating sweets. This simply is not true. No child is born with a need or a craving for sweets, but is introduced to them by adults or other children. Parents can, and should, start their children on healthy eating habits from infancy and prevent them from acquiring a sweet tooth.

My advice is to start this protective regime when children are about four months old. If you do not add sugar to foods when you start mixed feeding, your children will not begin to acquire a sweet tooth. If you do not add sugar to their food as they grow older they will have no desire for sweet things and will be happy to take a piece of fresh fruit rather than a sweet. If you do not give them sweet, fizzy drinks, they will, given the choice, prefer the more tangy, fresh fruit juices they are used to.

However, if you try to forbid your children to eat any sweets, you will probably end up in trouble. Complete denial simply means that your children will become furtive, will beg sweets from other children at school, and will scoff great amounts of sweets when they're available. I do think children should be allowed to have sweets occasionally. Most parents will probably work out their own rationing system, but if you care to adopt one, on pp. 97–8 I outline the one I used successfully with my four children.

You will find the book filled with information and advice of this kind. Based on sound nutritional theory and practical experience, it will help you to change to, and maintain, a healthy diet for your whole family.

Chapter 1

Out with the old, in with the new

There's no doubt that we are what we eat, so the greatest service we can do ourselves is to eat a healthy diet. We now know that much of what we learned in the past about a healthy diet should be discarded. For years we were encouraged to 'go to work on an egg' and 'drinka pinta milka day'. This kind of advertising is based on two things: accepted nutritional theory and commercial pressures. The first of these has been completely revised, and most of us no longer see the second as a reason to buy or eat anything. The fact is that the Egg and Milk Marketing Boards work on behalf of producers in their industries to maintain the price of their products and to prevent a glut. They represent the interests of their members – farmers – and the Department of Agriculture, but that's no reason for us to eat the wrong diet.

The old idea of a healthy balanced diet was based on the intake of large amounts of protein, and protein in the form of red meat and dairy products was particularly encouraged. A fairly high amount of either animal or vegetable fat was advocated because it is full of calories and provides energy. Fairly low amounts of carbohydrates were recommended because it was believed that they all were fattening and low in essential nutrients.

Our present state of knowledge on dietary needs turns this version of the healthy diet on its head. Instead of the high protein, moderate fat, low carbohydrate diet nutritional experts now propose a low protein, low fat, high carbohydrate diet.

The best information we have on what constitutes a healthy diet is the study by the National Advisory Committee on Nutritional Education (NACNE). Their report, *A Discussion Paper on Proposals for Nutritional Guidelines for Health Education in Britain* and better known simply as the NACNE Report, sets out to give realistic long- and short-term goals that we all can apply to our lives, enabling us to make changes from an unhealthy to a healthy diet gradually and painlessly. Its main themes, which I've summarized for you here, are based on our current national diet, which most authorities on nutrition agree is a disgrace.

These are the long-term goals and you shouldn't expect to achieve them in one fell swoop. I recommend

NACNE recommendations

Carbohydrates	We should increase our intake of carbohydrates by more than half, mainly by eating more unprocessed complex carbohydrates.
Protein	We should continue to eat the same amount of protein, but get more from vegetable and less from animal sources.
Fats	We should eat a quarter less fat, mainly by reducing our intake of animal fat.
Fibre	We should increase the amount of fibre in our diet by about half by eating more vegetables, pulses and whole grains.
Sugar	We should cut down our intake of sugar by half by eating fewer sweets and adding less sugar to food, coffee and tea.
Salt	We should reduce the amount of salt in our diet to about 5–9 grammes (0.2–0.3 oz) a day.
Alcohol	We should reduce our consumption by a third.

that you try to reach these goals gradually over the period of about a year. So that the changes aren't difficult, you might try making small alterations the first week. By the end of a month you probably will be used to them and can make further small changes and so on until you have reached the amounts of each nutrient recommended by the report.

Because the report is based on the amounts of different nutrients you eat, rather than specific food items, it's important to understand what those nutrients are, why you need them, and which foods provide them.

Calories

Food provides the body with energy, which is measured in calories, and nutrients – the basic elements it needs to grow, maintain itself, and function. The amount of fuel, or calories, you need depends on your metabolism, age, sex, size and level of physical activity. If you eat just the amount your body needs, all the calories will be used and your weight will remain stable. If you regularly eat more calories than your body needs, you will gain weight; if you eat less, you will lose weight. When planning your diet, you need to consider which foods provide the greatest quantity of nutrients for the number of calories.

Carbohydrates good and bad

A major function of carbohydrates is to provide energy, and in developed countries they account for 40 to 50 per cent of our calorific intake. There are two categories of carbohydrate, available and unavailable. The former includes sugars and starches, which the body can digest and metabolize. Unavailable carbohydrates are fibres, such as cellulose and pectin, which we cannot digest but which play an important part in the functioning of the digestive system.

In chemical terms the simpler carbohydrates, the monosaccharides, are the sugars. Many monosaccharide molecules link together to form the more complex polysaccharides, or starches. The body digests polysaccharides by splitting them down into monosaccharides, which it eventually converts to glucose, the body's main source of energy. Glucose is circulated to all parts of the body by the blood, and excess glucose is converted to glycogen and stored in the liver and muscles. When the storage capacity is full, any excess glycogen is converted to body fat.

Although both sugars and starches are important in maintaining the bulk and palatability of the diet, the body's ability to convert all carbohydrates to glucose means that sugar itself is not essential in the diet. However, the NACNE Report found that most of the sugar in the British diet comes in the form of sucrose, the refined white or brown sugar that is added to food and drinks. Sucrose is not a food and is totally unnecessary in the diet (see pp. 27–9). Most of us should be taking our sugar in the form of natural, simple sugars, such as fructose in fruit and lactose in milk.

Complex carbohydrates, which contain vitamins, minerals, protein and fibre (see pp. 26–7) as well as calories for energy, should form the healthy eater's

staple diet. They are found in most plant foods – cereals
and grains, fruits, vegetables and legumes – and are particularly useful to us in their natural state. When carbohydrates have been highly refined and processed, in
foods such as breads, cakes and biscuits, for example,
they are high in calories but have had most of the nutritional components removed. That is why they, like
the sugars, are called 'empty' calories. These carbo-
hyrates do not contribute to a healthy diet, but certainly
contribute to make us fat.

It might be surprising, but complex carbohydrates are
also the slimmer's best friend. A potato weighing 100
grammes (3.5 oz), for instance, if boiled or baked and
eaten with its skin, contains only about 75 calories,
which is about the same as a banana. It's only when we
fry it or add a good dollop of butter that its calorific
value shoots up. And a potato eaten with its skin has the
advantage of providing useful dietary fibre as well as
protein and vitamins.

The mighty proteins

Protein is contained in every living cell in the body – the
skin, blood, nerves, organs, muscles and bones. It is the
essential building material used in the manufacture,
maintenance and repair of our bodies, and helps
regulate all the body's functions.

Protein is made up of chemical units called amino
acids. There are about twenty-two amino acids, which
join up into long chains in varying numbers and

combinations to form an infinite variety of protein, each specific to a particular function. Thus the amino acid pattern of, say, blood protein differs from that of skin or muscle protein. The body makes some of its own amino acids and the rest come from our diet.

Our digestion and metabolism of protein converts the many types found in food into the specific ones needed by the body at any particular time. To achieve this, the protein is first broken down into its component amino acids, which then circulate in the blood. When they reach the tissue requiring new protein, they are reassembled in the appropriate patterns and proportions. Clearly the ideal protein food would be one that exactly matched the body's needs for amino acids, so that the protein requirement of each tissue could be met, but no such single food exists.

A healthy adult woman needs about 45 grammes (1.5 oz) of protein each day, and a man about 56 grammes (2 oz). Obviously there are many foods able to supply the required amount. Most of a loaf of bread eaten with a complementary pulse food, for example, could provide a day's quota, but that is hardly an appetizing thought. We have to eat a variety of foods not only for the sake of our taste buds, but also to ensure we are getting the right balance of other nutrients.

Animal and vegetable sources
Although meat is a high-protein food, we now know that with the exception of fish, fowl and white meat, it contains too much animal fat (see pp. 24–5) to be given

Protein content of common foods

	g/100 g	g/oz
Cheese, hard	26.0	7.4
Peanuts	24.3	6.8
Chicken	20.5	5.8
Beef and other lean meats	20.3	5.8
Liver	20.1	5.7
Cod	17.4	4.9
Eggs	12.3	3.5
Bread	7.8	2.2
Peas	5.8	1.6
Natural yoghurt	5.0	1.4
Milk	3.3	0.9

high marks in the modern healthy diet. Even if we cut off the visible fat, we should not eat a great quantity of red meat or fatty pork because of the invisible fat it contains. Farmers have bred animals to have what is called 'marbled' meat, meaning the meat has streaks of fat running through it to keep it moist during and after cooking. The recommendation for the modern healthy diet is that we don't eat red meat more than twice a week, and even then treat it as a 'condiment' – in other words, eat small amounts of meat with large quantities of vegetables, brown rice, wholewheat pasta, and so on. If you want meat on the other days, choose fish, poultry or rabbit.

We must remember that there are alternative foods that are more nutritious than almost everything we've been trained to regard as necessary. When we look at the nutritional quality of proteins from their amino acid pattern, it appears that vegetable protein can be just as good for us as animal protein. This eliminates the old idea of animal protein being first-class and vegetable protein second-class. In fact, different food proteins are complementary and offset each other's surpluses and deficiencies in amino acid pattern. Thus the amino acid patterns contained in bread and cheese, for example – the good old cheese sandwich – complement each other, as do those in a number of other traditional combinations, such as rice and pulses. It can be seen immediately, however, that unless you eat a wide variety of foods, the amino acid deficiencies of one food cannot be made up by another.

If we don't feel meat is necessary, we can get our daily protein requirement from pulse vegetables, including peas and the many varieties of beans that are now available; from eggs, as long as we don't eat too many yolks; and from cheese, provided we eat the lower fat ones, such as cottage cheese and the harder Swiss and Scandinavian cheeses.

Fats

Although fats occur in foods in several forms, the most important and abundant are the triglycerides, which are composed of chemicals called fatty acids and glycerine. Each molecule of glycerine can combine with three fatty acid molecules, which may be all the same or any of forty different ones. This accounts for the great variety of fats found in nature. Other types of fats found in foods are phospholipids, such as lecithin, and steroles, such as cholesterol. Food fats as a group are often referred to as lipids.

The main function of fats in the diet is as a source of energy. In most developed countries fats provide 35 to 50 per cent of a person's total energy intake, or calories. Although there is no physiological need for this much, fat does help to reduce the bulk of food that has to be consumed to meet energy requirements. It is also important because it carries fat-soluble vitamins, provides the body with essential fatty acids (EFA), and maintains the palatability of food, which anyone who has followed a low-fat diet knows.

There is no recommended daily intake for fats, but almost every world authority on diet agrees that we should eat less. The American Heart Association, for example, suggests that we should reduce our total fat consumption to about 10 to 15 per cent of our calorie intake if we have heart trouble, and to 20 to 25 per cent just to maintain health.

Fat content of common foods

	g/100 g	g/oz
Vegetable oils	99.9	28.3
Lard	99.0	28.1
Butter	82.0	23.3
Margarine	81.0	23.0
Mayonnaise	78.9	22.4
Peanuts	49.0	13.9
Cheese, hard	33.5	9.5
Pastry	27.8	7.9
Sardines	13.6	3.9
Fruit cake	11.0	3.1
Ice cream	8.2	2.3
Ham	5.1	1.4
Beef, lean	4.6	1.3
Milk, whole	3.8	1.1
Bread	1.7	0.5
Cod	0.7	0.2

Saturated and unsaturated

Most of the experts advise us to change the type of fat we eat, from saturated to unsaturated and polyunsaturated fats. In a saturated fat molecule all the carbon atoms are linked to the maximum number of hydrogen atoms. This makes the fat solid at room temperature. Most animal fats are of this kind, so saturated fat and animal fat are often used loosely to mean the same thing. However, fat from poultry and fish is unsaturated in spite of coming from meat and being solid at room temperature.

Because all the carbon atoms in an unsaturated fat molecule are not attached to the maximum number of hydrogen atoms, the fat is liquid at room temperature. Most vegetable fats are of this kind, so unsaturated fat and vegetable fat are often used synonymously. An exception is coconut oil, which is a saturated fat even though it is a vegetable fat and liquid at room temperature.

The Western diet, and particularly that in Britain, is biased towards saturated, animal fats. We eat only very small amounts of unsaturated fat, probably less than 10 per cent of our total fat consumption. Some experts believe that unsaturated fat, particularly of fish origin, may play a protective role in heart disease. Since Americans were given information on how to eat a healthier diet, particularly a heart-healthy diet, ten years ago, the national death rate from heart disease has fallen drastically. The United States is now fifth in the world's most improved table for heart disease, having climbed nearly twenty places. In contrast, the British as a nation seem to have ignored all the information on improving their diet. We still lie very near the bottom of the world table; Scotland enjoys the doubtful privilege of having the worst record in the world for deaths from heart disease; and Glasgow is the heart disease capital of the world.

Eating less fats of all kinds means adopting a few new habits: grilling food rather than frying or, if you have to fry, stir-frying the Oriental way, using a polyunsaturated vegetable oil such as sunflower oil or corn oil; eating less meat and choosing lean meats; using less cream and cutting down on whole-fat milk or replacing it with skimmed milk; cutting down on butter to just a scrape on bread and replacing it in cooking with a polyunsaturated vegetable fat; choosing low-fat cheeses. There are quite a few low-fat cheeses, including low-fat versions of some traditional higher fat cheeses. Many shops and supermarkets now label the fat content of meats and cheeses.

Cholesterol

Cholesterol is a type of fat that is found naturally in the human body and in certain foods. It is necessary because it is the starting substance for several hormones, including the sex hormones in both men and women. However, high blood cholesterol has been linked to a high incidence of heart disease. Eating less cholesterol-containing foods and less animal fat can lower the blood cholesterol and may reduce the risk of heart disease. For this reason most experts recommend eating less of these foods, particularly eggs and some of the fatty fishes, such as salmon and shellfish.

Fabulous fibre

Unavailable carbohydate (see pp. 16–17) includes celluloses and hemi-celluloses present in many plant tissues, pectin in fruit, and lignin in woody plants. As they cannot be digested by the stomach, these substances, known as roughage or dietary fibre, pass through the digestive system almost unchanged. Because it is not absorbed itself, fibre absorbs water in the intestine, which makes the stools soft and bulky, and speeds up the passage of food through the digestive system. This is obviously important in the prevention and treatment of constipation and other digestive disorders.

The importance of fibre was largely ignored until about twenty-five years ago when it was discovered that primitive communities that had a high-fibre diet, particularly those in Africa, had a much lower incidence of gastro-intestinal cancer than did people in Western nations, who ate very little fibre. Further research showed that the value of fibre is greater than we'd ever expected. Scientists now believe that it is possible that high levels of some types of dietary fibre might reduce the risks of some forms of colonic cancer and have a beneficial effect on deep venous and coronary thrombosis.

As a result, the fibre-is-good-for-you campaign began.

It is based on other good evidence too. When we as a species were still primitive animals, we made a kill and ate meat about once a week at most. Meanwhile we lived on root vegetables, berries and other fruits, all of which contain a large amount of fibre. So our digestive system evolved to cope and thrive on it. Ignoring fibre means ignoring an evolutionary imperative.

Dietary fibre occurs in all foods of plant origin, but the most important sources are whole-grain cereals, fruits, starchy roots such as potatoes, and pulses such as peas and beans, and nuts. However, the type of fibre present differs from one group of foods to another. Fibre in cereals, for example, contains a much higher proportion of hemi-celluloses than that in vegetables and fruit and is thought to be more effective than that from other plants in preventing and treating digestive disorders. Bran is the outer coating of wheat grains and contians the fibre. Since whole-wheat flour products made with it, ranging from bread to pasta and pastries, and whole-grain breakfast cereals contain all the bran portion of wheat, they are the most convenient ways of ensuring sufficient fibre in the diet.

Sugar

No one needs to eat sugar. It provides no nutrition whatsoever, so it's not necessary to health. We don't need it for energy either because we get enough calories from other foods that provide nutrients as well. Sugar, whether white or brown, crystalline or syrup, is a

Sugar content of common foods

	g/100 g	g/oz
Boiled sweets and candies	86.9	24.7
Honey	75.4	21.4
Jam	69.0	19.6
Raisins	64.4	18.3
Milk chocolate	56.5	16.0
Fruit cake	43.1	12.2
Sweet pickle	32.6	9.3
Sponge cake	30.9	8.8
Muesli	26.2	7.4
Biscuits, sweet	24.1	6.8
Peaches, canned	22.9	6.5
Ice cream	19.7	5.6
Fruit yoghurt	17.9	5.1
Coca-Cola	10.5	3.0
Baked beans	5.2	1.5
White wine, medium	3.4	1.0
Tomato soup	2.6	0.7

redundant food and is the greatest single cause of tooth decay.

Each man, woman and child in Britain consumes about 38 kilogrammes (84 lb) of sugar a year. One teaspoonful contains 75 to 80 calories. If you multiply that amount by how much you take each day in tea, coffee, other beverages, sweets, cakes and biscuits, you can see how it adds up and how many empty calories you consume – calories you might not burn up, which will then be deposited as fat. All of us, therefore, could benefit from taking less visible sugar and cutting down on invisible sugars. Invisible sugars are found in most processed foods, particularly canned and packet soups, sauces, pickles and spreads, so read food labels carefully. Remember that fructose, dextrose, maltose and glucose are other names for sugars. If any sugar is among the first three ingredients on the label, which are listed in descending order of weight, buy an alternative product.

Salt

In the last ten years it has been discovered that people with high blood pressure could reduce it by up to ten points simply by cutting down on the amount of sodium in their diet. We get some sodium naturally in our food, but most of it comes from the sodium we add in the form of sodium chloride, or salt.

The average person in Britain and America consumes between 12 and 24 grammes (0.4–0.8 oz) of salt a day.

This is far more than we need in a healthy diet. The National Institute of Health in America has recommended that Americans should try to reduce their salt intake to about 5 to 6 grammes (0.2 oz) a day, and the NACNE Report advises a daily maximum of 9 grammes (0.3 oz).

To achieve this most of us will have to adopt new habits. For example, we should use a minimal amount of salt in cooking and resist the temptation to add salt to food after it's prepared – so take the salt off the table. We need to look out for invisible salts, which are found in most processed foods. We should read the food labels again. If we see salt, soy, or any item with the word 'sodium' in it among the top ingredients, we shouldn't buy that product. This also means avoiding heavily salted foods such as salted nuts, crisps and almost any of the popular nibbles.

This doesn't mean that cooking has to be uninteresting. By using fresh herbs in our cooking we can bring out the natural sodium content and after a short period of adjustment no one will miss the salt. I did this with my family about eight years ago. After an initial two weeks during which they had to get used to new tastes, none of them has gone back to adding salt, and they all find foods cooked outside the family too salty.

Minerals

Calcium

Calcium is important because it makes bones and teeth hard and strong. It is also concerned with normal blood clotting, the transmission of nerve impulses and the digestion of milk in babies. Because it is instrumental in bone formation, our calcium needs are highest in childhood, but even in adult life there is a continual removal and replacement of bone calcium. Individuals differ considerably in the amount they absorb from food. The recommended daily allowance is 800 milligrammes per day for an adult person. Both pregnant and lactating mothers require about 400 milligrammes more. Although milk and its products are the richest source, calcium occurs in smaller quantities in many other foods, such as fish, bread, pulses and nuts.

Foods providing 200 mg calcium		
Cheese, hard	30 g	1 oz
Sardines	60 g	2 oz
Yoghurt, low fat	115 g	4 oz
Milk	170 ml	6 fl oz
Bread, white	225 g	8 oz
Peanuts	340 g	12 oz
Cabbage, cooked	450 g	16 oz

Iron

Iron forms part of the red pigment of the blood called haemoglobin, which carries oxygen from the lungs to the tissues and carbon dioxide, the waste product, in the opposite direction. Haemoglobin accounts for about half the total amount of iron in the body, the remainder being stored in various body tissues.

A healthy adult woman needs between 12 and 18 milligrammes of iron a day, and on average normal intakes reach these levels. The body stores regulate how much iron is absorbed from the food. If body stores are low, absorption will increase; if they are high, absorption will decrease. However, despite this and the presence of iron in many foods, some women still suffer from anaemia. Often it is caused by increased iron losses, for example, during heavy or prolonged periods, rather than low iron intakes. The symptoms of anaemia

Foods providing 6 mg iron		
Liver	30 g	1 oz
Beef	115 g	4 oz
Eggs	2	–
Apricots	140 g	5 oz
Bread, wholewheat	200 g	7 oz
Peas, cooked	480 g	17 oz

are a general lack of vitality and paleness of the skin, lips, tongue and inner lining of the eye. Iron supplements in the form of pills and tonics are an inexpensive and effective treatment, but only under medical supervision. Many people, however, have lower than normal haemoglobin levels without any symptoms of anaemia and iron supplements have little or no effect in these cases.

Other essential minerals

Sodium, potassium and chloride are important in enabling cells to absorb nutrients from the body fluids, and the balance between sodium and potassium is particularly important in maintaining the correct distribution of body fluids. They are all so widely distributed in food that it is impossible not to get enough of them. Individual variations in sodium intake largely depend on the amount of salt added to food.

Magnesium and phosphorus are essential to many body functions, and again occur so widely in foods that deficiencies are rare. Magnesium deficiency can arise but only from metabolic conditions that cause large magnesium losses, such as chronic diarrhoea or alcoholism.

Iodine forms part of the hormone thyroxine – secreted by the thyroid gland in the neck – which is important in the control of the metabolic rate. Iodine intakes are generally adequate except in areas where water, soil and therefore locally-grown food have a low iodine content. Such an area in England is Derbyshire, hence the name Derbyshire Neck for a goitre, the symptom of iodine deficiency. Seafood is usually the richest dietary source of iodine.

Fluoride is found in water, although in varying concentrations, and in some foods including seafood, tea, coffee, soybeans and rice. It is needed to form the hard bones and the enamel on teeth in childhood, and its continuing consumption reduces the likelihood of dental decay.

Vitamins

Vitamin A

Vitamin A is sometimes known by its chemical name, retinol. It occurs in food in two different forms, as retinol itself and as carotene, which the body can convert to retinol. The former is found in animal fats and the latter in green and yellow vegetables.

Vitamin A has many functions in the body, including maintaining the fine membranes that line all the body tubes and as part of the pigment in the retina that enables the eyes to see in dim light. An adult woman needs about 750–800 microgrammes of vitamin A a day and a man, about 1000 microgrammes. Because this vitamin is soluble in fat rather than in water, it can be stored in the liver, which means that two or three good meals a week that are rich in vitamin A are just as good as a smaller daily intake.

In developed countries an excess of vitamin A is a more common problem than a deficiency, usually as a

Foods providing 250–300 mg of vitamin A – one-third of daily needs		
Liver	7 g	¼ oz
Butter	15 g	½ oz
Carrots, cooked	30 g	1 oz
Margarine	35 g	1¼ oz
Eggs, large	1	–
Cheese	75 g	2½ oz
Milk	415 ml	¾ pt

result of an overdosage of concentrated vitamin preparations such as halibut liver oil. Too much vitamin A is toxic and can even be fatal, so it's vital to follow prescribed doses exactly.

Vitamin B

What used to be called the vitamin B complex has been broken down into eight B vitamins – B_1, B_2, niacin, B_6, B_{12}, folic acid, pantothenic acid and biotin – some of which are important in human nutrition and some of which are of rather obscure value. The B vitamins are soluble in water and therefore cannot be stored in the body. Moderately excess amounts are simply excreted in urine.

The five major B vitamins play an important part in the metabolic processes that release energy from carbohydrate, so people who eat significantly more carbohydrate will also need more of these vitamins. Fortunately, many foods that are rich in carbohydrate, such as cereal and bread, are also fairly rich in vitamin B_1, or thiamin. It's also present in pork and its products, in the watery residue of milk and in vegetables. In an average diet the loss of thiamin during cooking is around 25 per cent, but its fairly wide distribution means that a varied diet is the best insurance against a deficiency, which is rare in well-nourished populations.

Vitamin B_2, or riboflavin, is similarly present in a wide variety of commonly eaten foods, such as milk, white meat, liver, kidneys, cereals, eggs and vegetables. Some riboflavin will be lost during cooking and it can also be destroyed by light (bottled milk standing on the doorstep in bright sunlight can lose 10 per cent of its riboflavin content every hour). A deficiency of riboflavin in the diet can cause lesions on the lips, tongue and skin, but is extremely rare.

The third B vitamin concerned with the release of energy from carbohydrate is niacin. Like vitamin A, it is found in food in two forms, as the vitamin itself and as an amino acid called tryptophan, which the body can convert to niacin. Meat, especially liver, is the most important source of this vitamin, which is less affected by heat and light than the other B vitamins, although there are some losses when chopped or minced foods are cooked in water. A normal varied diet easily provides

Foods providing one-third of daily needs of the major B vitamins			
Vitamin B₁ (0.3 mg)	Nuts	30 g	1 oz
	Pork (lean)	60 g	2 oz
	Liver or kidney	115 g	4 oz
	Bread, white	170 g	6 oz
Vitamin B₂ (0.5 mg)	Liver	20 g	¾ oz
	Cheese	100 g	3½ oz
	Eggs	2	–
	Milk	380 ml	13 fl oz
Niacin (6 mg)	Nuts	20 g	¾ oz
	Liver	60 g	2 oz
	Meat, any kind	140 g	5 oz
	Bread, white	140 g	5 oz

sufficient niacin to meet an adult's needs and deficiencies are virtually unknown in the Western world.

Vitamin B_6, or pyridoxine, is involved in the metabolism of amino acids, so the amounts needed are linked to the proportion of protein in the diet. It is present in a variety of foods, including whole-grain cereals, meat, milk and fish, and a deficiency is rare. However, in the second half of the menstrual cycle, the high production of oestrogen speeds up the use of pyridoxine, and this relative deficiency has been linked with premenstrual depression.

Folic acid plays a part in the prevention of anaemia and in the renewal of all the cells in the body. Although it is present in a variety of foods, supplements of it are occasionally given during pregnancy, when needs can increase.

Vitamin B_{12} is also concerned with the prevention of anaemia and occurs only in foods of animal origin, so deficiencies can arise in people following strict vegetarian diets unless they take a supplement.

Vitamin C

The nutritional function of vitamin C, or ascorbic acid, is in the formation and maintenance of collagen, the substance that in effect sticks the cells of the body together. The now rare deficiency disease, scurvy, results in this connective tissue breaking down. Vitamin C is also involved in producing hormones, healing wounds, maintaining blood vessels and forming haemoglobin.

Authorities disagree over how much vitamin C we need. One school of thought believes that body tissue should be saturated with the vitamin, while another considers a lower level of intake quite adequate. Since both levels are well above that at which scurvy occurs, these arguments are of little practical value and most people's daily intake falls somewhere in between. In

*Foods providing 25 mg vitamin C
– half a day's needs*

Blackcurrants	15 g	½ oz
Sprouts	30 g	1 oz
Mustard and cress	30 g	1 oz
Cabbage	40 g	1½ oz
Orange	60 g	2 oz
Grapefruit juice	60 g	2 oz
Melon	85 g	3 oz
Turnip, cooked	100 g	3½ oz
Peas	115 g	4 oz
Lettuce	180 g	6½ oz
Potatoes, cooked	225 g	8 oz
Banana	250 g	9 oz

*Raw, unless stated otherwise.

recent years, vitamin C has received a great deal of publicity because of claims that regular very large doses could prevent colds, but as yet there is no reliable evidence for this theory. Generally, because vitamin C is water soluble, any moderate excess is lost in the urine. However, there are some indications that taking massive doses of 5 to 6 grammes a day can cause kidney stones and affect bone metabolism deleteriously.

Vitamin C is less widely distributed in food than, for example, the B vitamins, and fruits and vegetables are the only foods to make significant contributions to total intake. Even here there is a great variation in vitamin C content, as the table on p. 39 shows.

Even moderate sources of vitamin C can be import-ant to the overall diet if they are eaten regularly in sufficient quantities. In a standard diet, for example, potatoes can provide up to a third of an average vitamin C intake.

Vitamin C losses during the preparation, cooking and storage of fruits and vegetables can be considerable and overcooking can result in low intakes. Root vegetables can lose up to 50 per cent of their original vitamin C content during cooking (see p. 70).

Vitamin D

This vitamin is now sometimes called cholecalciferol. It differs from the other vitamins in that it can be made in the skin by the action of ultraviolet rays of the sun and in many cases does not have to be eaten at all. The amount of vitamin D acquired in this way is extremely difficult to estimate, as it depends on the length of exposure and the amount of melanin (brown) pigment in the skin. It is probable that white-skinned people with some daily exposure to the sun meet the body's needs for vitamin D, while dark-skinned people or people who do not expose their skin – for example, by their means of dress or by never going outdoors – will need a food source. Vitamin D helps the body absorb calcium and phosphorous from food and ensures that these minerals are used properly in bone and teeth formation. This means, of course, that it is especially important for babies and children, but it is also necessary for adults, as the mineral part of bone is constantly being renewed. A lack of vitamin D causes rickets in children and osteomalacia in adults. Both of these diseases are uncommon in well-nourished populations, but occur where the diet is low in vitamin D and exposure to sunlight is limited. Vitamin D becomes crucial again at the end of life when, along with calcium supplements, it may stave off osteoporosis (softening of the bones) particularly in women.

Vitamin D is a fat-soluble vitamin and can be stored in the liver. It is found naturally only in fatty fish, such as herring, salmon, pilchards, sardines, and in egg yolks. A weekly serving of a food rich in vitamin D is generally adequate for adults if combined with some exposure to the sun. In some countries it is also added by law to margarine, milks and baby foods to ensure that children, and pregnant and lactating women can meet their needs.

Other vitamins
In the body vitamin E, or tocopherol, helps to maintain and protect all membranes. Over the years it has been

claimed as a miracle cure for almost everything, very largely without supporting scientific evidence. It is found in many foods and a deficiency is unknown in human beings.

Vitamin K is vital to blood clotting. It is present in plant food and is manufactured by bacteria normally found in the human intestines. A deficiency is rare, but it is occasionally found in newborn babies, who may not have the necessary intestinal bacteria.

Who needs supplements?

Generally no one who eats a well-balanced, varied diet needs mineral or vitamin supplements. Among the few exceptions are total vegetarians who do not eat any animal food, very young babies, pregnant women – particularly those in their teens – and people with certain chronic illnesses. Many minerals and vitamins are needed only in microscopic quantities. The old adage 'If a little is good for you, more is better' is dangerous. In some cases when they are taken in large quantities, the excess is harmlessly excreted from the body, but in other instances the excess can be detrimental to health. It's been well known for years that excessive quantities of calcium, vitamin D and iron are toxic, and more recently it has been found that prolonged dosing of vitamin B_6 at too high a dose also can be toxic and produce very serious side effects. It's my conviction, therefore, that you should never take vitamin or mineral supplements without first consulting your doctor, and then take them only in the dosage he prescribes. Self-medication in this area is extremely hazardous, especially in pregnancy or if there is an underlying or chronic medical condition.

If your doctor prescribes supplements, you can buy them from the chemist. There is a widespread belief that chemically manufactured, or synthetic, vitamins are of little nutritional value and that only natural vitamins extracted from food sources (by chemical processes) are useful. In fact, there is no difference between them in chemical structure or the way in which the body uses them.

Now that you know what nutrients you need and why, let's look at the best ways of getting them.

Chapter 2
Putting theory into practice

Changing from an unhealthy to a healthy diet is not difficult; it simply involves making some different choices and emphasizing certain foods. It does require a little effort and determination, but once you start, you'll really enjoy it, feel marvellous and be encouraged to continue.

Most of the foods you should eat are easily available and, contrary to what you might have thought, you can eat more of some of them than in the past. You will soon find that a healthy diet can be delicious and satisfying. It doesn't involve starvation pangs, which would only lead to excessive snacking and over-eating later. In fact, you'll find that your desire to snack will gradually decrease and that eating a healthy diet helps you to control your weight without effort.

Making changes

Eat more	Old diet	New healthy diet
Poultry	900 g (2 lb)	1.125 kg (2½ lb)
Offal	115 g (4 oz)	170 g (6 oz)
Fish	565 g (1¼ lb)	1.125 kg (2½ lb)
Fresh potatoes	4.5 kg (10 lb)	6.8 kg (15 lb)
Fresh green vegetables	3 kg (6½ lb)	4.5 kg (10 lb)
Citrus fruits	450 g (1 lb)	900 g (2 lb)
Bananas	340 g (12 oz)	675 g (1½ lb)
Apples	900 g (2 lb)	1.8 kg (4 lb)
All other fresh fruit	565 g (1¼ lb)	1.36 kg (3 lb)
Dried fruit and nuts	340 g (12 oz)	675 g (1½ lb)
Brown bread	450 g (1 lb)	1.125 kg (2½ lb)
Whole-grain bread	225 g (8 oz)	2.25 kg (5 lb)
Other whole-grain cereals: rice, pasta, noodles	900 g (2 lb)	1.8 kg (4 lb)

Eat the same	Old diet	New healthy diet
Canned vegetables	1.125 kg (2½ lb)	Read the labels and buy only low-salt, low-sugar varieties
Other vegetable products	340 g (12 oz)	Try to eat more cooked dried beans and fewer chips
Canned fruits	225 g (8 oz)	Read the labels and choose low-sugar varieties
Fruit juices	560 ml (1 pint)	Buy unsweetened varieties
Preserves, jams and marmalades	225 g (8 oz)	Buy low-sugar varieties
Flour	565 g (1¼ lb)	

Eat less	Old diet	New healthy diet
Butter	365 g (13 oz)	255 g (9 oz)
Margarine	450 g (1 lb)	310 g (11 oz) – high in polyunsaturates
Oils, lard	365 g (13 oz)	255 g (9 oz) – only oils high in polyunsaturates

Eat less	Old diet	New healthy diet
Eggs	14	10
Beef, veal	900 g (2 lb)	540 g (1⅕ lb) – lean only
Mutton, lamb	450 g (1 lb)	310 g (11 oz) – lean only
Pork	450 g (1 lb)	310 g (11 oz) – lean only
Bacon, ham	725 g (1¼ lb)	400 g (14 oz) – lean only
Sausages, meat pies, processed meats, tinned meats, pâté	400 g (14 oz)	200 g (7 oz)
Sugar	3 kg (7 lb)	565 g (1¼ lb)
Sweets	900 g (2 lb)	450 g (1 lb)
White bread	2.4 kg (5¼ lb)	1.125 kg (2½ lb)
Biscuits	675 g (1½ lb)	450 g (1 lb)
Milk	18 l (16 pt) full-fat	9 l (8 pt) full-fat or 18 l (16 pt) skimmed
Other breads, fruit loaves, rolls, cakes, buns, pastries	765 g (1¾ lb)	380 g (14 oz)

The charts on pp. 46–8 shows how changing to a healthy diet affects what you eat on a monthly basis. As you'll see, the largest list is of foods you can eat more of. Don't try to make a sudden, great change; just make small ones gradually.

Food groups

Eating a balanced diet requires that you eat as wide a variety of wholesome food as possible. Food is traditionally divided into groups according to its nutritional content. Although these groups appear distinct when drawn on a chart, there are considerable overlaps between them; butter, for example, is both a milk product and a food high in fat. Generally, you should eat something from each group every day. Here are some guidelines to help you make your choices.

Cereals and grains

This group includes wheat, oats, barley, rye and rice, and the foods made of them, such as bread, pasta, biscuits, and breakfast cereals. Whole-grain products are the most nutritious and contain a lot of dietary fibre. Increase the amount of whole-grain foods you eat.

---

* Choose wholemeal pasta and unrefined brown rice.
* Eat about four to six slices of wholemeal bread a day.

---

* Buy unsweetened breakfast cereals.
* Use wholemeal flour for making pastry.
* Eat fewer cakes, biscuits and pastries even when they are made with wholemeal flour because of their high sugar content. Choose scones, currant buns, fruit and nut cakes and malt loaves, which are lower in sugar than cream-filled and iced cakes.

Fruit and vegetables

Fresh fruits and vegetables provide lots of vitamins, minerals and fibre. Eat more of them and a greater variety.

* Eat more potatoes. Try them thinly sliced and steamed, or boiled or baked in their skins, and eat them with low-fat yoghurt and herbs rather than butter. Mashed potatoes are tasty made with skimmed milk or low-fat yoghurt and parsley, seasoned with freshly ground pepper.
* Eat more salads of all kinds: try bean, corn, potato, celery and apple, carrot, bean sprout, beetroot, rice, and chick pea as alternatives to the familiar lettuce, cucumber and tomato.
* Use fresh fruits as your snack food and try a greater variety – have you tasted mango, papaya, passion fruit, ugli fruit, or kiwi fruit? Eat whole

fruits rather than drink fruit juices, and avoid squashes and cordials, many of which contain only fruit flavours.

* Choose a variety of yellow vegetables, beans and pulses, and green leafy vegetables each week. Put less salt on all your vegetables and steam or reduce the boiling time for green vegetables.

* Eat fresh, unprocessed nuts as snacks and put them in salads. Nuts contain essential fatty acids not found in many other foods, and therefore are a vital part of your diet. They are also high in calories, so don't eat too many, and avoid the roasted, dry roasted and salted ones.

Meat, fish and eggs

The foods in this group provide protein, vitamins and minerals, but you need to make careful choices because some of them also contain substantial amounts of fat. Cholesterol is found only in animal foods; generally, the more animal fat a food contains, the higher the level of cholesterol. Egg yolks, offal, red meat, sausages and other processed meat products are particularly high in cholesterol.

* Eat smaller quantities and only the lean cuts of beef, lamb and pork. Cut off all the visible fat and grill or roast rather than fry. When you're making

gravy, let the meat juices stand for a few minutes and then remove the fat from the top. In the same way remove the fat from the top of stew before serving.

* Eat less canned and processed meat and fewer meat pies. Buy low-fat sausages or get them from a butcher who will show you what goes in them.

* Choose poultry as an alternative to beef, lamb and pork. Before you grill, roast or stir-fry it, cut off all visible fat and remove the skin – most of the fat in poultry is under it.

* Eat more fresh fish and shellfish of all kinds. Fish is one of the healthiest foods, containing substances that are believed to reduce the risks of heart disease. Grill, bake, poach or fry in a little vegetable oil, and don't buy packets of frozen fish in fatty sauces.

* Eat no more than three or four eggs a week, including those used in cooking and baking. The egg white contains no fat, some protein and lots of minerals, so use it freely in mousses, soups and sauces, or hard-boiled in salads.

Milk and milk products

Dairy products are an excellent source of protein, vitamins and minerals, but they also supply 31 per cent of all the fat and 41 per cent of the animal fat you eat. The valuable nutrients of milk are not in the fatty part, but in the watery part.

* Buy skimmed or semi-skimmed milk and use it for drinking, pouring on cereal, adding to tea and coffee, and in cooking. If your milkman doesn't offer skimmed milk, write to your dairy and insist on it – you can.
* Start giving your children semi-skimmed milk after the age of six months and when they are weaned on to a mixed diet.
* Ask canteens to provide skimmed milk for tea and coffee.
* Use dry skimmed milk powder rather than coffee whiteners, which are made of vegetable fat.
* Spread butter thinly on bread and do not put it on cooked vegetables.
* Use vegetable oils rather than butter for frying.
* Eat more low- and medium-fat cheeses.
* Buy low-fat natural yoghurt rather than full-fat, sweetened or fruit-*flavoured* varieties. You can always add fresh fruit yourself.

Fats and sugars

As you've already seen, fats and sugars provide little nutrition and you should try to cut down on the amount you eat. Some foods in the other food groups are naturally high in fat and sugar, but the amount added in cooking or at the table is also a major concern. Of course, you do need some fat in your diet, so choose the healthier vegetable fats.

* Use less fat in cooking by grilling rather than frying.
* If you need to use fat, don't use lard or dripping. Choose margarines and cooking fats that are labelled 'high in polyunsaturates'.
* The best oils are sunflower, safflower, corn or maize, soya, walnut and olive. Avoid blended or mixed vegetable oils.
* Choose low-sugar varieties of jam and buy unsweetened rather than sugar-coated breakfast cereals.
* If you add sugar to cereals, tea or coffee, use only half the usual amount.
* Drink pure fruit juice instead of fizzy drinks and squashes.
* Have fresh fruit at the end of a meal and make a pudding only occasionally.
* Read food labels for hidden sugars.

To help you plan a balanced diet the chart on pp. 55–6 shows how many servings you should have from each food group every day. There can be a considerable variation in the nutritional value of foods within a food group, and where I feel these differences are relevant I have given a note in the far right-hand column of the chart.

There might be some foods in any group that you or other members of the family are allergic to (see pp. 151–3) or greatly dislike. In that case you can use the

food classifications to find alternatives. Similarly, if you
have to exclude a category of food from your diet – for
example, if you are a vegetarian you can use the chart to
see which other foods provide the same nutrients as

A healthy, balanced diet

Cereals and grains

Daily servings for an adult	4 or more. At least 4 slices bread *or* 115 g (4 oz) nuts *or* 225 g (8 oz) cooked pasta
Main nutrients provided	Protein, carbohydrate, calcium, iron, vitamins B_1, B_2, niacin
Points to note	Whole-grain cereals also provide fibre. Cereal-based foods made with sugar and fats, such as cakes, biscuits and pastries, have high-calorie and low-nutrient content.

Fruit and vegetables

Daily servings for an adult	4 or more. At least 1 orange *or* 115 g (4 oz) cooked green vegetables
Main nutrients provided	Iron, minerals, vitamins A, B, C
Points to note	Raw or lightly cooked fruit and vegetables also provide fibre. Citrus fruit, berries, currants and green vegetables are richest in vitamin C.

Meat, fish and eggs

Daily servings for an adult	2 or more. At least 90 g (3 oz) meat *or* 115 g (4 oz) fish *or* 2 eggs
Main nutrients provided	Protein, phosphorus, fat, iron, vitamins B_1, B_2, niacin
Points to note	Liver and kidneys are much richer in iron, vitamins B_1 and B_2, and are a good source of vitamin A. Fatty fish and eggs are also good sources of vitamin D.

Milk and milk products

Daily servings for an adult	2. At least 300 ml (½ pt) milk *or* 60 g (2 oz) cheese
Main nutrients provided	Protein, fat, calcium, vitamins A, B_2
Points to note	Cream, butter and cream cheese are low in protein and very high in fat.

Fats

Daily servings for an adult	30 g (1 oz)
Main nutrients provided	Fat, vitamins A, D
Points to note	Margarine is a richer source of vitamin D than butter. Cooking fats and oils contain few vitamins.

meat and fish. On pp. 58–9 is a list of just a few possible alternatives for some of the more common problem foods.

Should we eat the traditional English breakfast?

Breakfast is a very important meal, but many people rush through it, eating very little, and some go straight to school or work without eating anything. To give you energy to start the day and to help your body burn calories efficiently, it's better to eat a large meal early in the day than late at night. After all, calories consumed in the morning can be burned off during the next twelve hours, while the majority of calories eaten in the evening have very little opportunity of being burned off while you sleep. However, the traditional English breakfast of bacon, eggs, sausages, fried bread and fried tomatoes is not the bastion of good health we thought it was, even though it includes foods from most of the food groups. It's an unhealthy meal because it's extremely high in fat, and should not be eaten more than once or twice a week.

It is possible to have a very satisfying and nourishing cooked breakfast. As an alternative to bacon, you can have poached haddock, additive-free kippers, fish fingers or fish cakes. You can eat two or three eggs a week, but instead of frying them, boil, scramble or poach them and don't add butter. Eat fresh wholemeal bread with polyunsaturated margarine, and have fresh or grilled tomatoes instead of fried ones.

Alternatives

For:	Substitute:
Bread	rice pasta whole-grain cereals peas beans pulses potatoes in their skins
Green vegetables	redicchio celery leaves sprouting vegetables
Root vegetables	apples pears oranges bananas grapefruit
Citrus fruit	fresh fruit juice carrot juice tomato juice
Meat	fish eggs beans peas sprouting vegetables cheese milk milk substitutes

For:	Substitute:
Fish	meat cheese eggs
Milk	yoghurt ice cream cottage cheese cheese custard egg custard milky rice pudding
Cheese	milk milk substitutes meat fish eggs
Eggs	meat offal, particularly liver fish milk

Porridge is a very healthy food that is too often ignored. It's the only food that has been proven in controlled experiments to lower the blood cholesterol. When you cook porridge, it has a rather sticky, gluey consistency. Believe it or not, this gluey substance passes into the bloodstream and attracts globules of fat, which stick to it very much as flies stick to a fly-paper.

A cold breakfast can also be nutritious. Start with an orange or half a grapefruit, or fresh fruit juice. Choose whole-grain cereals or muesli, avoiding those that have added sugar. Instead of adding sugar, try raisins, prunes, or chopped banana, and use skimmed milk.

Healthy foods

The best foods to eat are whole foods untouched by refining and processing methods. The human body has evolved to eat foods in this form, and you could say you are doing your body a disservice by taking food in any other form. That doesn't mean you have to become obsessive or fanatical about the sort of food you eat. It really involves more judicious choosing and buying, and cooking methods. With the exception of meat and certain foods, like bread, that need to be cooked to be edible, raw food is usually better for you than cooked food.

Some people believe that foods must be grown in an entirely natural way, fed on natural fertilizers and free of chemicals added to the ground or sprayed on the food to protect it from insects and disease. This is a belief, not a rule. The overriding aim of the developed countries should be to produce enough food in a healthy form to feed the world. In certain areas the use of artificial fertilizers and pesticides is mandatory if this aim is to be achieved, and I believe the concession is justified.

Additives

Whole foods, while having the advantage of not containing additives and preservatives, have to be eaten fairly quickly; they don't have a long shelf-life. But there's no need to get obsessive about additives either. There is reason on the side of adding the minimum quantities of food additives such as preservatives, and there isn't any evidence to suggest that you shouldn't eat any.

Although food additives are so numerous that it seems difficult to keep track of them, you can soon learn enough about them to help you decide whether they are there to preserve food or have been added to increase the sweetness or saltiness, or just to enhance the colour. Since January 1986 manufacturers have had to list additives on food labels not just by name, but also with an 'E' number. E numbers apply only to additives approved by the European Economic Community (EEC). Numbers without an E prefix are additives not yet approved by the EEC, although their use may be permitted by individual countries within it. Some of the major E number categories are:

permitted colours	100–80
preservatives	200–90
permitted antioxidants	300–21
emulsifiers and stabilizers	322–494
anti-caking agents	530–78

flavour enhancers and sweeteners	620–37
bleaching agents	900–27
modified starches	1400–42

The E numbers 212–17 are additives that are dangerous either to asthmatics or aspirin-sensitive people, and food containing these additives should not be given to babies or young children. There are also certain additives that are not permitted in baby and infant foods, and they are given as a separate list.

After reading food labels you might decide that you'll accept the additives because the food will be in better condition and better tasting than without it; or you might decide that you'll reject the product because the additives are being used to try to enhance lower-quality raw materials.

Health food stores

Although many people prefer organically grown, unrefined, unprocessed, whole foods, there is no evidence that any food you buy in a health food store is necessarily better for you than the same food bought elsewhere. Many people may prefer to shop there because the yoghurt is better quality, the nuts bigger and sweeter, the dried fruit softer and juicier, and the bread is the best in the district. These reasons are to be commended. But when individuals swear by the change in the quality of their lives or improvement in their health after eating foods available only in health food stores, it is important to remember that anecdotal reports do not constitute scientific proof, and cannot and should not be applied as rules.

There is also no evidence that some of the more esoteric products sold in health food shops are of any benefit whatsoever. Many are sold on the basis of ancient claims from distant cultures that they are endowed with magical health-giving properties. Included in this group are honey, cider vinegar, yoghurt, molasses, garlic, ginseng and buckwheat.

Usually such foods are promoted on the premise that because they are eaten by one particularly healthy population they will bestow health on another regardless of the other health factors in both populations. Yoghurt is a good example. It was reputed to be eaten by Bulgarian peasants who lived to a very ripe old age, and so was marketed in Western Europe and America as promoting long life. Honey has been credited with medicinal properties for centuries despite the fact that it is only sugar (glucose and fructose) and water. Cider vinegar, it has been claimed, will melt away unwanted body fat without the aid of a diet, and the newest recruit, ginseng, is currently gaining ground as the elixir of life. However, apart from the undoubted placebo effects, nutritionally such foods have no magical properties and don't do as much for health as a well-balanced diet.

Health food stores also sell an enormous range of herbal remedies and pills of simple, inorganic salts, which between them have probably claimed to cure just about every ailment known to man. There are various arguments against the self-administration of these products, the main one being that it may delay or even prevent a person from getting proper medical advice.

You should also bear in mind that such common substances as salt, sand and plaster of paris are marketed under unusual names at vastly inflated prices. The over-zealous use of herbal remedies can give rise to medical problems. The active substances are found only in very small amounts in plants and have to be extracted and concentrated before they are of any use pharmaceutically.

Getting started

You are now armed with the information you need to begin to change from an unhealthy to a healthy diet. To help get you on the right track, here is a list of a few good habits you should start to develop and a few bad habits you should ease out of your lifestyle. Choose only three or four points on the list to start. When you have incorporated them fully into your daily pattern, choose three or four more, and continue until you have worked through the whole list.

* Start saying **yes** to:
  fresh vegetables
  healthy nibbles, such as fresh and dried fruits,

raw vegetables like carrots and celery, unsalted nuts

bread and toast without butter or with just a scrape

grilled foods instead of fried

all kinds of salads.

* Start saying **no** to:

a lot of meat

salty food

sugary foods such as cakes, biscuits, sweets, fizzy drinks, puddings

fried foods

lots of butter and cream.

* Start reading food labels for hidden sugars and salts, additives, and fibre content.
* Start reading books on healthy eating and cooking.
* Start choosing:

wholewheat bread and pasta

low-calorie, high-fibre crispbread

potatoes in their skins

brown rice.

* Find the nearest shops with lots of different whole grains, beans and pulses.
* In restaurants choose healthy foods from the menu, such as uncooked starters like salads, fish or poultry instead of red meat, and simple garnishes instead of rich, fatty sauces.

* Start buying:
  skimmed milk
  low-fat cheeses
  low-fat sausages
  low-calorie salad dressings
  low-calorie food and drinks.
* Try to eat as a whole family so that you're not tempted to eat first with the children and then with your partner.
* Start to serve smaller portions on smaller plates.
* Stop watching television or reading while you eat, especially when you're alone. Give your whole attention to the food, be conscious of eating and what you are eating. This way you are less likely to over-eat.
* Start using sweeteners partly or wholly instead of sugar, especially in cooking.
* Compare the calorific values of different snacks if you are tempted to eat them – some crisps and chocolate bars have fewer calories than others.
* Start using bran instead of white flour to thicken soups, stews and gravies.

Keeping it going

You will probably be able to manage a healthy diet most of the time, but unfortunately you will still be left with the occasional craving. Image-retraining can help to overcome that. Researchers at Stanford University in the United States believe that overcoming a craving can be helped by conjuring up images that make the craved-for food seem less attractive. Let's say, for example, that you crave a big fat steak and chips. First get a basin of dripping or a block of lard from the refrigerator and look at it. Spoon some of it on to a plate and feel it with your fingers. Now you are ready to start the drill.

1 Find a quiet place and sit or lie down.
2 Get as physically and mentally relaxed as you can (see pp. 133–5).
3 Think of steak and chips – the way they look and smell, the overall picture.
4 Now think of the appearance and texture of the dripping that comes from the steak and chips.
5 Imagine that this thick fat is slowly working through your arteries.
6 Link the image of the food with the sludge in your arteries.
7 Now think of a less fatty but equally delicious food, such as turkey.
8 Link this image with clean, healthy arteries throughout your body.

Chapter 3
Good cooking = healthy eating

Healthy cooking is absolutely no different from good cooking. All cooking has a profound effect on the appearance, texture and taste of food as well as on its nutritional value. Good, healthy cooking means using certain methods and being careful not to overcook foods, so that they look attractive and retain the maximum nutritional value and taste. Vegetables should be still crisp, meat still juicy and no food should have its taste drowned in thick sauces and gravies.

Some loss of vitamins is inevitable during cooking, as the table on p. 70 shows.

A certain amount of these vitamins is lost however the food is cooked, but frying and boiling can increase such wastage considerably. The figures look terrible, but it's

Percentage of vitamins lost during cooking

	Vit B$_1$	Vit B$_2$	Niacin	Vit C
Cereals: boiled	40	40	40	–
baked	25	15	5	–
Eggs: boiled	10	5	–	–
fried	20	10	–	–
Fish: poached	10	–	10	–
fried	20	20	20	–
Meat: roast/grilled	20	20	20	20*
stewed	60	30	50	
Milk: boiled	–	10	–	30–70
Vegetables, leaf:				
boiled	40	40	40	70
Vegetables, root:				
boiled	25	30	30	40

*For liver only.

comforting to know that most normal diets still provide an adequate amount of vitamins. To avoid the unnecessary loss of vitamins, remember:

> * Do not chop foods finely and allow them to soak for a long time before cooking. This renders them almost vitamin-less.

* Do not cook any food for longer than necessary.
* Do not keep food hot or warm for a long time before serving.

Apart from preserving nutrients, cooking methods can play an important part in long-term health and weight control in other ways. For example, grilling, baking and poaching rather than frying can markedly reduce your fat intake, especially with foods such as onions, mushrooms, potatoes and bread, which soak up enormous quantities of fat when fried. Using a minimum of fat in cooking is not a health fad; it's one of the healthful aspects of cooking advocated by most nutritionists as well as *haute cuisine* cooks and gourmets. To help you cook healthily, here are some points about ingredients and methods that you can incorporate into your own style of cooking.

General ingredients

Sorting out the fats
Although there is a lot of emphasis on reducing the amount of fat in your diet, you still need to eat some and you might wonder whether to use butter or margarine. Many advocates of butter say that because it is a natural dairy product it must contain more goodness than margarine, but this simply is not true. Margarines are fortified with all the minerals and vitamins that occur

naturally in butter. Some people think that margarine is more slimming than butter, but that is not true either. Butter has 740 calories per 100 grammes (about 3.5 oz) and margarine has 730. The fats labelled 'low-fat spreads' contain fewer calories because they are made of half as much butter, margarine or other fats with the difference made up by water. Oils have more calories than butter and margarine – 899 per 100 grammes – because they don't contain water.

A good rule is to reduce *all* fats, particularly hard cooking fats like suet, lard and dripping. And you might want to consider whether you and your family need to eat butter or margarine at all. If you do want to continue spreading some fat on your bread, potatoes or vegetables, choose a polyunsaturated margarine rather than butter.

With so many different brands available, how can you know which margarine to use? In general, buy margarines that are labelled 'high in polyunsaturates' (see pp. 24–5) and avoid those that say only 'soft', 'made out of 100% vegetable oils', 'low in cholesterol', or 'blended/ mixed vegetable oils'. Whether you are buying margarine or cooking oil, don't assume that vegetable fats are necessarily good; some of them contain quite a lot of saturated fat. Palm oil and coconut oil are the only two vegetable oils that are saturated, but they often find their way into blended vegetable oils. As there is no way of knowing exactly what's in a bottle labelled simply 'vegetable oil', choose those clearly marked sunflower, maize or corn, sesame, soya, safflower, or olive oil. If the label suggests that the bottle might also contain other vegetable oils, don't buy it.

Use any oil only once for frying. It doesn't matter if the oil still *looks* good or if the manufacturer claims it can be re-used. What you can't see, and what is important to your health, is the chemical change: every time an oil – even a highly polyunsaturated one – is heated, it becomes more saturated, which is just what you are trying to avoid.

Hold the salt!

You know that the NACNE Report recommends that you eat less salt in order to reduce the amount of sodium in your diet (see pp. 29–30). Because sodium is a constituent of most natural foods except fruit, there is absolutely no nutritional need to add salt when you are preparing or serving food. The art of cooking without salt is to use alternative flavours provided, for example, by herbs, spices and lemon juice. Try this, and don't use any salt at all or gradually reduce the amount you use over a period of weeks. You'll probably find that your food hasn't lost any of its flavour, but if you are tempted to add salt, use just a tiny pinch.

It's important to remember that there can be a lot of 'hidden' salt in processed foods. Salted butter and margarine are obvious, but look carefully at food labels too for any additive that includes the word sodium, such as monosodium glutamate or sodium hydroxide. Baking powder, bicarbonate of soda, brine, and soy also indicate the presence of sodium. These are, of course, ingredients of such everyday items as self-raising flour, pickles, bottled sauces, and stock cubes, as well as many canned vegetables and processed (including smoked and canned) meats, sausages and fish. Cut down your intake of products that have salt as an essential ingredient, like pickles, and look for the low-salt or no-salt-added varieties of others, for example, unsalted butter or margarine and canned vegetables.

Don't be so sweet

For the sake of your figure and your health – particularly your dental health – eat less sugar. Although artificial sweeteners are an alternative to sugar, it is better to try to wean yourself from sweet tastes completely. It's possible to reduce the sugar content in most recipes by at least half without changing the nature of the dish, and if you do it gradually, you'll find that you quickly become accustomed to 'sharper' flavours.

Creative ways with . . .

. . . Fish

* If you really want to fry fish, use a polyunsaturated oil instead of butter.
* Season fish with lemon, dill or fennel and bake it with onions.
* Steam fish with spices and onions, Chinese-style.

* Put the fish into a pan, nearly cover it with skimmed milk and flavour it with black pepper, nutmeg and bay leaves. Bring to the boil so that the milk rises over the fish, then cover, lower the heat and simmer until cooked.
* Brush a little oil on both sides of the fish and grill it without turning. Grill mackerel and sprats with a little French mustard.
* From the cheapest (e.g. herring) to the most expensive (e.g. salmon), fish can be cooked in foil. Season with fennel or dill, chopped parsley, shallots, pieces of tomato and lemon slices. Smear French mustard inside herrings. Add 2 fluid ounces of water and a little dab of margarine. Bring the edges of the foil together and seal. Cook in a moderate oven for about 45 minutes.

. . . *Vegetables*

* *Steaming* Use a minimum of water, and put a firm lid on top of the pan. The vegetables will retain a lot of their flavour, goodness and original colour.
* *Boiling* Always bring the water to the boil before immersing vegetables, boil them for as short a time as possible and take them out still firm.
* *Stir-frying* Cut the vegetables into thin slices, so that each piece can cook through quickly. Never use large chunks, or they may be overcooked on

the outside and undercooked on the inside. Put a tiny bit of oil in the bottom of a wok or frying pan and cook the vegetables for only a few minutes over a hot flame, stirring them all the time. They will have a sharp taste and a crisp texture.

* *Sautéing* Use any combination of vegetables, such as finely chopped cabbage, carrots, cauliflower, parsnips, onions, mushrooms, courgettes, peppers, marrow, celery and apples. Fry the vegetables in a very little oil for about 30 seconds, add stock or tomato juice and bring to the boil. Put a tight-fitting lid on the pan and allow the vegetables to cook themselves for 5–8 minutes. Sprinkle with grated Parmesan cheese and serve with rice or an omelette.

* Cook some vegetables, such as leek and spinach, in their own juice. You don't need water; just put a little oil in the bottom of the pan to stop the vegetables from sticking.

Try to think about using vegetables as main courses rather than accompaniments. For example, make main-course salads, soups, stews and stuffed vegetables, such as peppers stuffed with minced meat or rice and mushrooms, tomatoes stuffed with spinach and cheese, and so on. Serve these with cheese, rice, pasta, eggs or potatoes.

... Beans and pulses

In India, China, Latin America and all through the Middle East beans are an essential part of the diet. They are usually made fragrant with spices and cooked in stews, eaten with rice or made into salads. Fermented beans, succulent bean curd and fresh bean sprouts are included in all meals.

One reason why beans are so popular in poor countries is that they are a cheap and excellent source of protein and can provide a great deal of variety. Many people in the West are familiar with only a few ways of using pulses – we eat mushy peas, split-pea soup and baked beans – but there are many more imaginative meals to be made from peas, beans and lentils of different kinds.

Beans are so simple to prepare. All you have to do is to wash them, soak them overnight, then bring them slowly to the boil in fresh water and simmer until tender. When the beans are soft enough to crush between your finger and thumb, or between your teeth, they're done. A quicker way of cooking pulses is to bring them to the boil slowly, simmer for five to ten minutes, remove from the heat and allow to cool for an hour, then bring them back to the boil and cook until tender.

The cooking time varies greatly and depends largely on when the pulses were harvested and how long they've been in store. As a general rule, lentils take between 35 minutes and 1 hour, beans take 1½ hours and chick peas may take 3 hours or longer.

Using beans and pulses

Split yellow peas	Their most famous use is in Swedish yellow-pea soup, flavoured with thyme, marjoram, ginger, bacon, onions and cloves. It is eaten every Thursday in Sweden in memory of King Eric XIV, who died on a Thursday in 1577 after his brother had slipped poison into his yellow-pea soup.
Split green peas	These are the peas used in pease pudding. They are also tasty made into a soup flavoured with mint or thick Dutch soup flavoured with smoked sausage or frankfurter, and they're often made into a purée to serve with cold meats, usually pork or ham.
Small lentils	These can be mauve, black, white, green, mottled, yellow, pink or orange; there are more than sixty varieties. They can be boiled as a vegetable to serve with game, pork or rabbit; made into a lovely spiced soup; or curried.
Brown lentils	These are larger than the lentils described above and more robust. Their flavour is excellent, though they are a little floury in texture; sprinkled with finely chopped parsley, they make a very good accompaniment for ham, pork or lamb. Be careful when you're cooking with oil because they soak up large quantities.

Split lentils	These small, bright orange or yellow pulses are excellent for making dahl, which is served with curry. They cook quite quickly to a mushy consistency, but they're rather tasteless without plenty of spices.
Egyptian brown beans	The traditional way to serve these is to season them with oil, lemon and garlic, sprinkle them with chopped parsley and garnish them with hard-boiled eggs, halved or sliced.
Aduki beans	This bean is known as the prince of beans throughout the East. It has a sweet flavour and in China is used to make a soup that is served in a tall glass with grated ice and cream, like a knickerbocker glory. The beans are also made into a cream similar to a chestnut purée, which is used as a filling for wedding cakes.
Black-eyed peas	These are used a great deal in America's Deep South and are traditionally served with pork or dried ham and candied sweet potatoes. They have a delicious flavour that goes particularly well with spinach, ham and garlic.
Lima beans	These are usually white or an attractive pale green. Used a great deal in American cookery, they are a substitute for haricot beans in soups, purées and salads and are delicious with sour cream.

Black beans	These are a great favourite in Caribbean cooking. In Cuba they are served with a mixture of cumin, onions, red pimentos, cider vinegar and a hot tomato sauce, often mixed with rice. In the East they are fermented, then cooked with slivers of chicken, ginger, garlic, soy sauce and shallots.
Red kidney beans	The Mexicans use them in *chilli con carne* and, 're-fried' or mushy, as an accompaniment. In Italy they are made into a soup with garlic and sage, and in Spain they are eaten as a main course served in a tomato sauce with rice.
Soya beans	These are the most nutritious beans of all: half a cup of soya beans is equivalent in protein to a medium-sized steak. They can be boiled like haricot beans or sprouted like mung beans, and they provide oil, flour, soya-bean curd and soya sauce.
Brown borlotti beans	These are used for making soup and have a creamy consistency. They can also be used in *minestrone*. They're often cooked with ham bones, onions and cinnamon, short noodles and plenty of grated Parmesan cheese.
Butter beans	These are the familiar beans of school meals and are very unattractive if served simply boiled. Instead serve them in fresh tomato sauce flavoured with celery.

Chick peas	These need to be soaked for at least 24 hours, then boiled and simmered for at least 3 hours, often longer. They can be eaten on their own as a snack, added to chicken stew or crushed and mixed with sesame-seed paste, lemon and oil.
Mung beans	These are primarily sprouting beans. To sprout them, soak the beans overnight in cold water, drain them, place them on a tray so that the air can circulate freely, then cover them with a wet cloth and put them in a dark place. Sprinkle the beans, tray and cloth with water every morning and evening to keep them moist, and in five or six days you'll have bean sprouts.
Haricot beans	These are used a great deal in French cooking and often served with a *gigot* of lamb cooked with garlic and a sprig of rosemary. You can also make a sauce by crushing a few spoonfuls of cooked beans and adding tomato paste. Don't use fat to moisten them; just add some juice from the meat.
Pearl beans or small haricots	These are the original baked beans, traditionally cooked with salt pork, brown sugar or molasses and a pinch of mustard – no tomatoes. If they are baked all day in a deep earthenware pot, sprinkled with brown sugar half an hour before they're ready to come out of the oven and allowed to caramelize, they can be a delicious accompaniment.
Flageolets	These delicate pale-green beans have a subtle flavour. They can be cooked and eaten whole or made into a purée, decorated with chopped parsley.

Most beans will cook within 1 hour in a pressure cooker.

---

* If you don't have time to plan ahead, don't buy the dried beans that need soaking overnight. Ask in the store where you buy them which beans need the least soaking. There are some, for instance, over which you simply pour boiling water and leave for about 45 minutes before cooking. Lentils and black-eyed peas (which are really beans) can be cooked immediately, without soaking.
* When cooking beans and pulses, put a tiny lump of margarine or a little oil in the pot for lubrication.
* The longer pulses and beans cook, the less flavour they tend to retain, so flavour with herbs or spices before serving.
* *Always* throw away the water in which beans and pulses have been soaked or boiled.

... *Sprouting seeds*

Sprouting your own seeds is a job that's fun for all the family, especially children. In as little as five days, even in winter, you can grow your own food, packed with goodness. As soon as sprouting begins, the level of many vitamins and minerals increases by as much as 1000 per cent, especially vitamin C; the carbohydrate content drops and the protein value improves, so these are among the healthiest foods you can eat.

You can get sprouting seeds, with instructions on how to sprout, from almost any health food store. Among the ones that we like best are wheat, sunflower, alfalfa, peas, lentils and mung beans. You can eat them raw, when they're best, or cooked as a garnish for soups or stews and in soufflés. You can blend them into sauces, sandwich spreads and meat and nut loaves, and they can be added to almost any dish at the last moment for crunchiness and nutritional value. You can even add them to your bread dough.

. . . Potatoes

* *Boiled* Scrub the skins clean with a hard brush. Don't peel the potatoes, or if you can't eat the skin, peel only after cooking.
* *Steamed* Slice the potatoes thinly and steam them with onions and parsley or other herbs.
* *Mashed* Mash potatoes with skimmed milk, polyunsaturated margarine or yoghurt and chopped onions, chives, parsley or garlic. Add freshly ground black pepper before serving.
* *Baked* Baked potatoes eaten with their skins on provide fibre, starch, vitamins and minerals. Instead of butter, use a very low-fat cheese or yoghurt as a filling and add chives or other herbs.
* *Fried* If you make your own chips, use the firmest potatoes you can find and cut them into very

> large chips so that, in proportion to volume, there is less surface area to soak up fat. Fry the chips in a polyunsaturated oil.

... *Meat*

The most saturated meat fat comes from beef and lamb, followed by pork, then poultry and game, so buy meats in the reverse order of frequency. Always ask your butcher to cut off the fat and not to include fat in a rolled joint. Before cooking, cut off any remaining fat that you can see and remove the skin from poultry.

* Choose unsmoked bacon, which contains less salt than smoked bacon, and buy the leanest cuts. Cut off any excess fat before cooking, and grill bacon rather than frying it.
* Use half the usual amount of meat in stews and casseroles, and make up the bulk with vegetables.
* Before you serve a stew or casserole, let it cool so that you can skim most of the fat off the top.

... *Desserts*

My children were always asking for a pudding, and I was at my wits' end trying to ring the changes. Instead of racking your brain every day for something new, try thinking about puddings in a different way. Here are some ideas to get you started.

* Mixtures of freshly cut fruit – say, banana, apple and orange.
* Mixtures of fresh and dried fruit: apples and dried apricots; bananas and sultanas; prunes and fresh peaches; apples and dates; and so on.
* Mixtures of dried fruit soaked in pure orange juice so that they're not too dry or tough, mixed with a crunchy cereal.
* Stoned prunes filled with curd or cottage cheese. Fresh or dried figs and dates can be used too.
* Stoned prunes wrapped in lean bacon and grilled.
* Cubes of cheese and pineapple or apple on cocktail sticks.
* Ice lollies made with fresh fruit juices, milk or yoghurt.
* Half a banana frozen with a stick in it and coated with melted chocolate for a special treat.
* Cubes of pineapples on a stick, dipped in honey or shredded coconut and eaten as they are or frozen.

. . . Biscuits and cakes

* Use half the amount of sugar listed in recipes, or try using part sugar and part honey. (Remember that honey is sweeter.) You could also use artificial sweeteners, some of which provide their own recipe books.

* Reduce the total amount of fat that you use in baking and use polyunsaturated fats – most recipes will work with these instead of animal fat.
* Always use whole-grain flour in place of all or part of the specified quantity of white flour. Experiment a little to find out which proportions you and your family like best.
* Enrich the flour that you use with soya flour or wheatgerm to improve the protein content of a cake or tart, or try this combination: for every 225 g (8 oz), substitute 1 tbsp soya flour, 1 tbsp powdered skimmed milk, 2 tbsp cornflour and 1tbsp wheatgerm, and make up the rest of the quantity with the flour of your choice.
* Dried fruits contain lots of minerals and improve the nutritional value of cakes and biscuits. They're also sweet, so they allow you to reduce the amount of sugar in the recipe. Always wash them first to remove the liquid paraffin from the surface.

. . . Healthy drinks

* Use a juicer or liquidizer to make drinks from a variety of fresh fruits or vegetables and water.
* You can try your hand at a large range of natural fruit milkshakes, nut milks and blended fruit drinks.

* Soak raisins or dried apricots and apples in a lot of water overnight to make a sweet juice to drink in the morning.
* Instead of chocolate or cocoa, blend a little carob flour with milk or water.
* Use a medicinal herb drink as a base and flavour it with herbs and spices. Children's favourites are aniseed, fennel, ginger, cinnamon, mint, lemon balm, lavender and meadowsweet.
* Try drinking herb teas occasionally. You can buy a wide variety or make your own from borage, rose petals, marigold, thyme, spearmint, pepper-mint, coltsfoot, basil, aniseed, sarsaparilla, rosemary or sage.
* Try karina, a bitter-sweet lemon drink. Sprinkle a tiny amount of sugar in a small pot of boiling water, then pour it over slices of lemon. The longer you let it stand, the more bitter the drink will be.

Chapter 4
Your children's diet

Once eating habits are established, they're not easily changed. The best way to ensure that your children eat a healthy, balanced diet for the rest of their lives is to help them develop good habits from the beginning. This is more than a matter of simply presenting them with healthy food. Children need to enjoy mealtimes and find food interesting. In this chapter I discuss principles that apply to all children, and then examine the different needs of specific age groups.

Mealtimes

You should try to make every mealtime happy, relaxed, pleasant and friendly. It is one of the best times for children to help and to get used to being members of the household team. From about the age of two and a half, for example, a child can help to lay and clear the table. Every mealtime is also an opportunity to teach children about cleanliness, tidiness, discipline and table manners. Children learn by imitation, so be careful to set a good example. Resist any impulse to deliver lectures on nutrition or scoldings about food left uneaten, and don't allow mealtimes to become a battlefield or source of friction. I feel that it's very important for the entire family to meet at a meal at least once a day if possible. It helps children to learn about and enjoy one of our most pleasant social activities – eating together – and have contact with their parents and each other. It should not be interrupted by television, video, reading or other activities, which defeat the purpose of being together and distract attention from eating properly.

Children can become noisy and irritated if they are kept waiting too long when they sense that the food is ready, so call them to the table only when the meal is going to be served. This means remembering that young children nearly always prefer their food lukewarm rather than piping hot, and allowing time for it to cool before serving. Make the seating arrangements, utensils and crockery as easy as possible for children to use. If possible, always eat when your children eat, and eat the same food. If they are quite young and you must eat food that is different, then try to eat it at another time.

Attitudes to food

Encourage chiildren to regard food as something to be explored, played with and enjoyed, not as a solemn subject served with a lecture on what they should and should not eat. If children can't identify the food they're eating, they tend to be suspicious and might refuse to eat a particular food for a long time. The more you involve them in buying, preparing and cooking the food, the more likely they are to eat it. And these are the times when you can find opportunities to teach children not only about good nutrition, but also about numbers, colours, textures and tastes. When you teach your children about food, stress the positive aspects and say 'do' more often than you say 'don't'.

Often children will not respond to your teaching, advice or cajoling the first time. Don't lose heart; be patient and repeat your advice. Set a good example by eating the food you tell your children is good for them. Try to change a food habit only if you think that to continue it will lead to poor nutrition, but never try to force children to eat a particular food that they don't like. No single food is essential and you can always find an alternative that is just as nourishing and that your children will like. As a rule children prefer bland foods to spicy ones, so don't challenge their palates too soon.

Always remember that children have small appetites, small stomachs and less interest in food than you do, but need to eat more often. Several small meals a day are more suited to their small stomachs than a few large ones. A good rule of thumb is that the younger the children, the more often they should eat, and the more often they eat, the smaller the meals should be. On average, young children eat five to seven times a day, which means that some meals can be thought of as snacks. They start to eat fewer and larger meals as they get older. The number of times a day your children eat is not important; what they eat is. Plan all the meals and snacks for a day at one time so that you can be sure they offer lots of variety and each contributes to the daily nutritional requirements.

Eating problems

Every child, even when a baby, will dislike certain foods. I don't believe in camouflaging such a food by mixing it with another or bribing a baby to eat a spoonful of it by promising a spoonful of a food he likes, actions that might lead him to dislike two foods instead of one. And the more worked up you get, the more your child will make a fuss; he'll quickly learn that it's a way of manipulating you. To help keep disliked foods to a minimum, introduce a new food when your child is really hungry and therefore more likely to eat it. Remember that no single food is essential as long as you offer a wide variety of nutritious food, and that if your child dislikes a particular food, there is always an alternative that provides the same nourishment (see pp. 58–9).

Nearly all children have mild food fads from time to

time. For example, your child might suddenly decide he doesn't want to eat anything except fruit and yoghurt. After seven days, he might decide he doesn't want to eat anything except meat and potatoes. Just be patient. Don't spend time preparing food you know your child might refuse, and then feel resentful when he does. If a child senses that you are especially anxious for him to eat up his greens, for example, he might refuse simply as a way of expressing his independence. The more you nag him, the more determined to disobey he will become. Threats and bribes won't work either. If you do not let him have his pudding, which he does want, until he's eaten his greens, which he doesn't want, you turn mealtimes into an emotional battlefield and may establish a dislike of greens that will last a lifetime.

Once an eating problem exists, it takes time and patience to get rid of it. You need to relax so that the child no longer feels under pressure. Then he can give his attention to his appetite. Start with small portions of the foods he likes best. Put the plate in front of him. If after half an hour he's not eating, just take the plate away and resist the temptation to tell him he's naughty or to cluck in disappointment. Don't allow him to fill up on unhealthy snacks or sweets before the next meal; he will not go without food long enough to come to any harm.

Sometimes a child refuses to eat because he's not hungry at the time you serve the meal. Think back; perhaps it's a day when you've served quite a number of snacks, or the child has just had a lot of vigorous exercise. A child will often refuse to eat if he's not feeling well. Is he rather pale, fretful and mummyish? If so, check his temperature, and always get the doctor's advice if you are worried. If your child refuses to eat for no apparent reason, be as casual as you can about it. Never try to force a child to eat just because it is a scheduled mealtime.

Weight problems

Very few children are underweight unless they are deliberately being deprived of food. Just like adults, some babies and children are naturally small and slender. Your child might weigh less than another child of the same age and sex and still be a healthy weight for his size and physique. If your child is eating a balanced diet and is happy and developing normally, you probably have nothing to worry about. If you are anxious, talk to your doctor.

Being overweight is nearly always caused by a poor diet combined with a lack of exercise. A fat child is invariably eating too many empty calories, usually in the form of cake, biscuits, sweets, ice cream and sweet drinks. If your child is becoming overweight, check his diet. Is he eating too much sugar? Ferret out the invisible sugars by reading the labels on packaged foods (see p. 29), and if you've been adding sugar to food, stop immediately. Use an artificial sweetener, if necessary, and gradually reduce the amount. Is he eating too much fat (see p. 23); for example, butter, fried foods, high-fat cheeses, fatty meat? Is he eating healthy snacks? Is he eating because he is hungry or because he is bored? Make sure your child is getting every opportunity to play and be active. Play with him yourself and encourage him to play with other children.

Problem foods

On p. 96 is a list of foods I suggest you avoid. These products won't necessarily harm your children, but they are low in nutritional value and may contain substances to which young children are sensitive or intolerant. None of them is essential and there are healthy alternatives for almost all of them.

I have already said that I don't recommend anyone to eat convenience foods, junk foods, or sweets. Of course, most parents use convenience foods now and then, and I agree that as an occasional part of an otherwise healthy diet they will do no harm. It is true that convenience foods save time on planning and preparation, require little equipment and minimum skill to prepare, and make it possible to serve different meals at the same time. However, you can make most of the same dishes yourself and they will probably cost less, taste better, contain no artificial additives, and have fewer calories and less fat, sugar and salt.

It is particularly difficult for children to avoid some contact with junk food and sweets when they are constantly advertised as good and fun to eat, and when they are offered by relatives, friends or other children.

Foods to avoid

Dairy products	Condensed or sweetened milk, processed cheeses, cheese spreads, sweetened yoghurt, cream substitutes, sweetened cream
Fats and oils	Lard, suet, blended vegetable oils, solid cooking fats and margarines, low-calorie margarines
Cereals and grains	All processed wheat products, including white flour, white bread, white pastry and white pasta; processed baking products such as cake or pudding mixes, gravy mixes, custard powder, frozen white pastry; all commercial breakfast cereals, white rice, nuts and seeds on their own or in sweets
Fruits	Fruit canned in heavy syrup, crystallized fruits, fruits frozen with sugar, canned fruit pie fillings, commercial fruit pies
Vegetables	Canned vegetables, especially those that have added sugar or salt (read the labels), baked beans and frozen vegetables. Restrict their use if you can't eliminate them completely
Drinks	All fizzy drinks, fruit squashes, lemon barley water, sugary blackcurrant cordials, hot chocolate drinks, commercial milkshake mixtures, alcohol
Meat, fish and poultry	Fresh, canned and frozen commercial processed meat products, including sausages, pâtés, meat pies, ham, hot dogs, meatballs, beefburgers, faggots, savoury pancakes, and frozen fish products in batter or heavy sauces

Although I know children don't need them, I believe it is wrong to try to deprive them of these foods. It is important for children to be accepted by their peers, and banning certain foods can make them feel like outsiders. It might lead them to eat the forbidden items secretively. Don't make your children feel guilty about wanting or eating such food, but make sure they understand that it should be eaten only occasionally. And remember, there are always alternatives that are healthier and that your children will accept. For example, you can now buy unsalted nuts and crisps, muesli bars with nuts and raisins, and carob-coated raisins and nuts.

I used a rationing scheme for sweets with my children. From the first time they had sweets, they were never allowed more than one and they had it only at a particular time of day. In the first instance it was after their evening meal – the after-dinner sweetie. When they reached school age they were allowed an after-lunch sweetie too. The sweet ration was not negotiable and because the practice started early in their lives the children never argued about it. When they said they were embarrassed or felt left out because they didn't have packets of sweets at school like the other children, I pointed out that eating a lot of sweets is unhealthy and particularly bad for their teeth, and I showed them my fillings. After that they seemed able to cope with whatever situations they encountered.

As they got older I allowed them more freedom to exercise their judgement. When they asked if they could have a sweet, I would say 'yes, and come and show it to me'. If they'd taken too many, I would remove a few, or if they'd taken a whole bar, I would cut it into pieces. By the age of eight or nine they were truly responsible. Now the eldest never eats sweets, the 16-year-old is not interested in them, the 14-year-old is happy with a sweet occasionally, and the 11-year-old never asks for them. If you have young children you may want to use this scheme as a model.

The first six months

A discussion of breast-feeding versus bottle-feeding would take many pages, and is already thoroughly covered in many books on baby and child care. The guidelines I give here apply whichever method you decide to use.

Most authorities now recommend that children are fed purely on milk up to the age of at least four months, although the practice in America has been to start babies on solids much earlier. The latest research has shown that the too-early introduction of solid foods can lead to intolerance and allergies. Furthermore, there is no logic to introducing solid foods before the baby's primitive gut can digest them, absorb them and therefore get nutrition from them.

Every baby is different, so how can you tell if your baby is ready to be weaned? A biological sign that your child is ready for solid food is the cutting of the first tooth, which can occur any time after four months.

Somewhere between four and six months you will notice that your baby's appetite is increasing markedly, and by six to eight months most babies are eager to have at least a little solid food. By this age they need a more varied diet because their rate of growth and development demands more energy, vitamins and minerals than can be supplied by milk alone. Don't worry if your baby shows very little interest in solid foods until after he's six months old. You can gain nothing by trying to force solid foods on a baby before he's ready for it.

Six months to one year

When you introduce solid food, whenever possible use food that the rest of the family is eating. In this way your child starts becoming familiar with part of the good balanced diet that he will be eating eventually. Your baby's food should not contain sugar or salt, so cook the meal for your family without adding either of these condiments. Extract little portions for your baby and then season the remainder to suit the tastes of the rest of the family. Of course, because a baby eats more often than older people, you will have to prepare some of his meals specially. Until your baby's teeth begin to appear, all his food should be soft enough to be sucked off a spoon.

To give your baby the first taste of a food, choose the morning or lunchtime meal when he is most hungry and offer the food before the milk. Put a tiny amount on the front of a teaspoon and let the baby try to suck it off.

Start with only tastes of food and never give more than a
teaspoon at the first sitting. When solids are accepted,
gradually increase the amount until they replace milk
as the baby's staple diet. Don't rush things. Even though
your baby's appetite increases, give him only very small
portions, as the young digestive system learns to adjust
from a milk to a solid diet only gradually.

Remember, too, that your baby needs a varied diet
even among his first foods. Most mothers start with
special baby cereals of rice, oats, or barley because they
are bland and, mixed with a little milk, taste very
similar to the baby's previous diet. Puréed fruit and
vegetables are totally new tastes that can surprise and
delight your baby and stimulate his palate. Try very
lightly boiled, puréed pear or apple, steamed, puréed
cauliflower or parsnip. For many babies a favourite food
is a teaspoonful of freshly grated carrot juice, squeezed
through a piece of fine muslin.

After your baby has accepted one or two solid foods,
you'll probably find that he will be eager to experience
more new tastes and textures. If one food isn't accepted,
don't make a fuss. Wait a couple of days and try again,
offering him a different food in the meantime. Don't
rush your child on to chopped, grated and minced food.
As soon as his teeth begin to appear the very bland, soft
foods will not be interesting enough for him.

When you introduce solid foods, your baby will not
drink as much milk as before and will need other fluids.
From the time solid foods form even a small part of your
baby's diet, satisfy his thirst with water and diluted

fruit juice, not milk. Milk is a food, not a drink. As you gradually increase the amount of solid food you give your baby over the next few weeks, he will be taking most of his calories from it and the amount of milk he will want will decrease further. You can't give him too much water because healthy kidneys will get rid of it.

Keep your baby's new diet as low in fat as possible, for example by not introducing butter and cream. In addition, you shouldn't give your baby any food or drink that is spicy, sugary, smoked, salted, or oily. Avoid shellfish, rhubarb, yeast extract and, of course, coffee, tea, and alcohol.

It's very easy to become emotionally involved in weaning, so try to keep a psychological distance between yourself and your baby during mealtimes. If you can, laugh at yourself a little and try not to spend too much time on preparing your baby's food or you will feel natural resentment when he rejects it. Don't teach your baby to try to please you, but to eat for his needs. Never force a child to eat anything. There is no food on earth that your baby absolutely must have.

Here are some guidelines for weaning recommended by most baby-feeding experts.

---

* Introduce new foods only one at a time and gradually.
* Don't try to introduce a new food when your baby is tired, suffering from teething problems or over-hungry.

* Never add cereal or rusks to a bottle feed.
* Don't give your baby juices, sweetened or un-sweetened, in a bottle. Offer small, well-diluted amounts on a teaspoon.
* Use a special drinking beaker to make the transi-tion from breast or bottle feeding easier. Be prepared for your baby to take a few weeks to get used to it.
* Don't introduce unmodified cow's milk until the age of one year.
* Except for very young babies, do not encourage eating at bedtime.
* It's very easy to choke when you cannot chew properly, so *never* leave your baby alone with food or give him raisins, currants, sultanas, fruits with seeds, nuts or sweets, which could all block the windpipe.
* Never use leftovers for a baby's food, and don't re-use cans or jars of food if a spoon has been dipped into them. Always give small portions of food, a teaspoon at a time, and throw away leftovers.
* Encourage self-feeding. From the age of about six months, babies will stretch out to try to help you to feed them, eventually taking hold of the spoon. This is especially important for babies who have a tendency to be overweight; they are less likely to overeat if they feed themselves.

The chart on pp. 104–5 gives some examples of how weaning might proceed.

From the beginning, meals should be fun. Remember that food isn't only for your baby to eat for nutrition, but it's to play with. Allow plenty of time to enjoy meals – make them as long and as fun-filled as you like. While children don't necessarily eat slowly, adults in general eat much too quickly and your natural inclination is to try to hurry the baby.

Feeding times will become messier as your child gets older, but don't worry about it. Put newspaper or a plastic sheet under the high-chair and table to catch the mess, and keep your baby well away from walls, unless they have an easily washable surface, because by now he can throw food. He might also smear food on his clothes, the high-chair and his face and head. This is an important part of the learning process.

After a month on solids your baby will have grasped the technique of getting food successfully off the spoon. By the time he's taking two solid meals a day he'll probably open his mouth when he sees the full spoon approaching.

When your baby is six to eight months old, or as soon as he is eating two or three small meals a day, he can eat with the rest of the family and enjoy small portions of the same food, minced, diced or mashed. Pull the high-chair up to the table so that the baby feels he's really part of the family and participating in the mealtime activities. Encourage him to think of himself as being an active member of the family group. Don't

Weaning programme

Around 5–6 months

Early morning	Breast or bottle feed as usual
Breakfast	2 tsp cereal, then a lightly boiled egg yolk, followed by a feed
Lunch	1 tsp puréed meat or fish with 3 tsp sieved vegetables. Try giving a drink of water or well-diluted fruit juice instead of the feed
Mid-afternoon	Mashed banana or other soft fruit as well as the usual feed
Late afternoon/ dinner	Give the breast or bottle feed if your baby is still hungry

Around 6–7 months

Early morning	Breast or bottle feed as usual
Breakfast	2 tsp cereal or porridge with some lightly scrambled egg. Offer some milk from a beaker or cup instead of the usual breast or bottle feed
Lunch	Try giving minced or mashed food instead of puréed food. Give meat or fish with some vegetables, then yoghurt and fruit and a drink of water or well-diluted fruit juice
Late afternoon/ dinner	A cheese or similarly savoury wholemeal bread sandwich, then fresh fruit and yoghurt; try giving milk from a cup instead of the usual feed

---

Around 7–8 months

Early morning	Offer a drink of water or fruit juice instead of the usual feed
Breakfast	Cereal, then a boiled egg with wholemeal bread, a drink of milk
Lunch	Cheese, fish, minced meat, chicken or liver with mashed vegetables, a milk pudding or fresh fruit, a drink of water or fruit juice
Late afternoon/ dinner	Wholemeal bread with a savoury filling, fresh fruit, and a drink of milk

Around 9–12 months

Early morning	Drink of water or fruit juice
Breakfast	Cereal, then bacon, egg or fish with wholemeal toast and butter, a drink of milk
Lunch	Chopped instead of mashed meat, fish or cheese, a milk pudding or fresh fruit, a drink of water or fruit juice
Late afternoon/ dinner	Meat or cheese sandwiches with a drink of milk

ignore him; chat to him occasionally, give him lots of glances and smiles, and praise him whenever he does something right or pleasing.

Very soon he will want to feed himself and will simply take the spoon from you. Be prepared to let your baby experiment and put up with the mess. Be encouraging and praise all attempts at self-feeding. It will give your baby a feeling of accomplishment and confidence, and will make mealtimes more enjoyable. It is also a huge step forward in your baby's development, helping him to become manually dexterous and to coordinate muscles and movements. Feeding himself will speed up the coordination of hand and eye faster than any other activity.

Your baby will take several months to become proficient at self-feeding. Don't worry if food seems to be too much of a plaything and most of it is on the floor – he won't go hungry. Around the time a baby starts to self-feed, the initial growth spurt is beginning to slow down, so he needs less food. It's wise to have a spoon each, one for you and one for the baby, until he can manage to get food successfully into his mouth. If he can't scoop food up on to his spoon, swap your full spoon for his empty one.

Here are a few tips to help you make feeding time easier on both of you.

* Tuck a pile of tissues under the neck of the bib to stop the baby's neck getting wet as he practises drinking.
* If your baby won't wear a bib, put a coloured scarf around his neck so that the clothes are still protected.
* If your baby is going to sneeze, get out of the way or you'll be covered in food.

* Fit a paper-towel holder over the back of the high-chair or near it so that you have supplies on hand for emergencies.

One of the most satisfying ways for your baby to feed himself is with finger foods – any food he is able to pick up and put into his mouth using only his hands. If the food is hard, your baby can suck it and experiment with chewing. It is important that a baby learns to chew properly before his first birthday. Chewing means that the food is well mixed with saliva, which starts the digestive process. It also helps jaw and jaw muscle development, both of which are important in learning to speak. Chewing stimulates blood flow to the jaw and gives nourishment to the gums and teeth, so some hard foods that encourage chewing should be part of your child's diet. Some useful foods are suggested below and on p. 108.

Finger foods

* *Protein foods* Cubes of soft cheese, macaroni and cheese, fingers of cheese on toast, scrambled eggs, cottage cheese, meat in pieces, chunks of firm fish taken off the bone, hard-boiled eggs in slices.
* *Fruit and vegetables* Cut any fresh fruit that is easy to hold into slices and remove the skin and any pips – bananas are one of the best. Any raw or

cooked vegetable that you can make into a stick
or other shape that is easy to grasp; for example,
carrots, celery, broccoli, mashed potato.
* *Grain and cereal foods* Small pieces of dried,
sugarless cereal, little balls of cooked rice,
wholemeal bread and toast with butter or margarine, wholemeal rusks without the complete
grains.

One to two years old

By now your child's diet should be presenting very few
difficulties in terms of cooking or special preparation.
He should be eating a good mixed diet, including plenty
of fibre and a wide range of foods. You will no longer be
cooking separately for your baby, as most of his meals
can be taken from those for the rest of the family. Most
babies enjoy the flavours of garlic, onions and herbs, but
remember to avoid using salt, sugar and spices.

Give your child at least one nutritious protein dish at
each meal and at least four servings of fruit or
vegetables a day. He'll be able to eat an increasingly
large amount of food at each meal. Exactly how much
depends on his size and rate of growth. He may be able
to eat a third to a half of a standard adult portion each
time, but don't worry if it is less. Milk – skimmed milk
– should remain an important part of your child's diet,
as it is a useful source of protein, but he should also be
given water and diluted fruit juice when he is thirsty.

A sample diet for an 18-month-old toddler

Day 1

Breakfast	1 scrambled egg ½ slice buttered brown toast 225 ml (8 fl oz) diluted orange juice
Mid-morning	225 ml (8 fl oz) diluted orange juice 1 sliced apple
Lunch	60 g (2 oz) white fish ½ brown bread roll 1 tbsp green beans 225 ml (8 fl oz) diluted fruit juice
Dinner	140 g (5 oz) baked beans 60–85 g (2–3 oz) potatoes *with* 60 g (2 oz) grated cheese on top ½ banana 225 ml (8fl oz) milk

Day 2

Breakfast	225 ml (8fl oz) diluted orange juice 115 g (4 oz) yoghurt 1 tbsp baby muesli ½ tbsp wheat-germ 60 ml (2 fl oz) milk ½ mashed banana
Mid-morning	225 ml (8 fl oz) diluted orange juice 1 biscuit
Lunch	225 ml (8 fl oz) milk 225 ml (8 fl oz) water 2 home-made fish fingers 1 tbsp peas

Mid-afternoon	225 ml (8 fl oz) water
Dinner	1 egg omelette *with* 30 g (1 oz) cheese 1 tbsp green beans 225 ml (8 fl oz) milk ¼ slice brown bread

Day 3

Breakfast	60 g (2 oz) cereal plus milk 225 ml (8 fl oz) diluted orange juice ½ banana
Mid-morning	225 ml (8 fl oz) water 1 peeled apple
Lunch	Egg florentine: 2 tbsp spinach, 1 poached egg, 30–60 g (1–2 oz) cheese 1 pear yoghurt (without sugar) 225 ml (8 fl oz) milk
Mid-afternoon	450 ml (16 fl oz) diluted apple juice 1 oat biscuit
Dinner	1 ham sandwich on wholemeal bread Cubes of cheese Raw carrot Cubes of melon

Day 4

Breakfast	1 poached egg, chopped up ½ slice wholemeal toast and peanut butter ½ peeled apple 225 ml (8 fl oz) skimmed milk
Mid-morning	115 ml (4 fl oz) diluted carrot juice 1 sugar-less wholemeal biscuit

Lunch	60 g (2 oz) chicken 1 chopped fresh tomato 1 potato in skin 1 home-made ice lolly of puréed fruit 225 ml (8 fl oz) water
Dinner	170 g (6 oz) wholewheat pasta *with* tomato and/or meat sauce 225 ml (8 fl oz) skimmed milk ½ banana

Day 5

Breakfast	1 tbsp muesli *with* 115 g (4 oz) plain yoghurt and chopped dried fruit ½ peeled pear 225 ml (8 fl oz) diluted tomato juice
Lunch	Cauliflower cheese ½ slice wholemeal bread 225 ml (8 fl oz) water
Mid-afternoon	225 ml (8 fl oz) skimmed milk Fingers of wholemeal bread and tahini
Dinner	1 home-made beefburger 1 tbsp carrot 1 tbsp green-leaf vegetable ½ mashed banana 225 ml (8 fl oz) milk

Day 6

Breakfast	Leftovers from last night's family dinner Fresh pineapple chunks 225 ml (8 fl oz) milk
Mid-morning	225 ml (8 fl oz) diluted apple juice ½ slice home-made poppy-seed cake

Lunch	Fingers of home-made pizza
	1 tbsp sweetcorn
	225 ml (8 fl oz) water

Dinner	170 g (6 oz) rabbit stew
	2 tbsp spinach
	1 peeled peach/plum
	225 ml (8 fl oz) skimmed milk

Day 7

Breakfast	115 g (4 oz) yoghurt with sliced fresh fruit
	½ slice wholemeal toast and tahini
	225 ml (8 fl oz) milk

| Mid-morning | 225 ml (8 fl oz) diluted grape juice |
| | ½ home-made scone |

Lunch	115 g (4 oz) home-made chicken or
	turkey rissole
	1 tbsp mashed swede
	½ slice brown bread
	1 tbsp ice cream
	225 ml (8 fl oz) water

Dinner	1 chicken-liver sandwich on wholemeal
	bread
	Fingers of raw carrot and celery
	2 tbsp home-made brown rice pudding
	225 ml (8 fl oz) water

He will be more skilled at feeding himself and will have a lot of control over his spoon, fingers and cup. He is ready to learn about good table manners too. Don't start by thinking that teaching good manners will be a problem. Always use a pleasant tone of voice and don't resort to slapping or punishment. Don't expect your child to obey your instructions immediately. Most children need to be told and shown what to do at least three or four times. It takes time for a child to realize that you mean what you say every time and he'll put your authority to the test. Even if he is slow to understand, never get cross or tense. Your child may feel that he's unable to handle the situation and simply revert to bad behaviour. Make your boundaries of good behaviour clear and your standards consistent, and remember to give lots of praise when they're adhered to. Your child will soon adopt the patterns that he knows will win your approval.

Around the age of one year your child will probably be crawling and trying to walk. It won't come as a surprise if he is unwilling to sit in his high-chair for a long time. If your child insists on getting down, let him do so. He'll come back for more food in a few minutes and will soon learn that food and eating mean sitting at the table. If your child doesn't show signs of coming back to the table, don't insist that the food is eaten.

By the time he is toddling, your child will eat three smallish meals a day with a snack in the morning and the afternoon. Be prepared for his appetite to be a bit erratic during this year; he may want very little one day and eat everything that you give him the next. Don't be alarmed even if he goes through periods of having a very small appetite; his body will prompt him to eat enough to meet its needs. Don't worry if your child goes on food binges either, eating only one food and refusing all others; it is perfectly normal at this age.

Two to three years old

Between the ages of two and three children tend to prefer dairy products like milk, yoghurt, ice cream, cottage cheese as well as breads and cereals. They also tend to dislike and may even reject meat, fruit and vegetables. Don't get very anxious about this. Instead, try to find a couple of meats and some fruits and vegetables that your child really likes and stick to them until he signals that he wants a change.

Your child's daily calorie requirements will continue to increase as he grows and during this year he'll need roughly 45–50 calories a day for every pound that he weighs.

Give your child two or three servings of protein foods and four or more servings of fruit or vegetables each day. Remember to keep portions small. You can give him second helpings if he is still hungry, but don't worry if he doesn't finish everything. Provide four or more servings of bread and cereal: a serving is half a slice of bread and one or two tablespoons of cereal. Always serve whole-grain bread and avoid high-calorie, starchy foods.

Eating patterns at this age change quite a lot and your child may have food fads throughout the year. He may also demand rituals at mealtimes. For example, he might insist on having his sandwich cut on the diagonal and refuse to eat it if it is cut in any other way. Some children want their plate set in a certain way and will throw a tantrum if it's not. The best way to approach such demands is with patience. After all, adults have food rituals too; we sit in certain positions at the table and we may prefer our tables set in a certain way. As long as your child's preference is reasonable, you should indulge the ritual. However, if it interferes seriously with his intake of food or disrupts the family, try to reason with your child and explain that such behaviour is not fair to others. In this way your child learns an important lesson in socializing. Be firm, but be prepared for it to take several attempts to break an undesirable ritual.

In this year your child will become quite familiar with the social aspects of eating, but don't expect too much. It's very difficult for a child to concentrate on eating with a spoon, not spilling his drink, not making a mess and being quiet while eating at the table with you. He's trying to listen to what you're saying, to participate in the conversation and to concentrate on the food. He's learning a great many new skills all at once, and it's not surprising that he gets excited. There are bound to be accidents, so be understanding and flexible.

Here are some tips that may help you to organize meals and snacks and make them fun.

---

* Try to involve your child in planning and, more important, preparing meals and snacks.

* Always make sure that a meal contains at least one food that you know your youngster likes.
* Always serve small amounts and allow second helpings. A large, piled-up plate is intimidating to a child.
* Keep food simple. Children like to see what they're eating; they don't like messed-up foods.
* Always offer a variety of foods to guarantee a balanced diet and to avoid boredom.
* Liven up your toddler's meals by using brightly coloured food.
* If your child wants to use a knife, give him a plastic or blunt-ended one and supervise him all the time.
* Raw fruit, juice and low-fat milk drinks are very nutritious and popular snacks. Let your child use a straw for drinking sometimes. So that he won't tip the drink over, cut the straw so that it protrudes no more than two inches above the cup or mug.
* Try to make snacks amusing. For example, make an open wholemeal sandwich that looks like a smiling face, or cut pieces of fruit into unusual shapes.
* Try to include a finger food in every meal until your child is going to school.
* Be open to innovation and occasionally serve your child's meal or snack on a doll's plate or on a flat toy.

* Serve some food in unexpected ways. Ice cream cones don't have to be used only for ice cream: you can fill them with a mixture of chopped cheese and tomato or tuna-fish salad. Yoghurt, which your child may not like straight out of the carton, becomes more like ice cream when you freeze it.
* Put lots of different finger foods, such as bits of cold meat, raw vegetable, fruit, potato and tiny smooth peanut butter sandwiches, into a cake tin and let your child pick out what he wants.
* Encourage your child to build his meal on some occasions – making, say, a car or a boat out of sandwiches, cubes of cheese, vegetables and dried fruit. When it's complete, he can eat it.

Three to five years old

Although, obviously, children are still growing, their *rate* of growth is slower than in infancy. This means they need slightly less food in proportion to their weight – roughly 36–41 calories a day for every pound they weigh. To meet their nutritional requirements children of this age should be eating the same number of servings of food from the four main groups as adults, although the servings will still be smaller. The chart on pp. 124–5 shows how much of each type of food they need, and ways of providing it.

Dairy foods supply an abundance of calcium, phosphorus and magnesium, which children need for strong bones and teeth, and usually continue to be popular foods at this age. Breakfast cereals, wholewheat bread, and fresh fruit and vegetables are also popular now, and provide iron and fibre. Many young children still don't like roast meat, chops or steaks, which are fibrous and take more skill and strength to chew than do chicken, fish and processed meats like beefburgers and sausages. To make joints more appealing roast them carefully so that they are not overdone but are soft and retain their natural juices. If you cook chops and other cuts of meat in casseroles, they will absorb some of the stock and become softer and easier to chew. And while children may not like calves' or pigs' liver, they often do like chicken liver. Remember too, that there are alternatives to meat, such as peanut butter, peas and the great variety of beans and cheeses.

It's not surprising that as children grow, their tastes change. It's usual for six- to seven-year-olds to like simple meats, potatoes, raw vegetables, milk and fruit. Some of the mixed foods they find acceptable are spaghetti and meat sauce, macaroni and cheese, and possibly pizza. At seven or eight, children are more likely to want to try new foods than when they were younger. Foods that they disliked at an earlier age may now become acceptable and they may show strong food preferences. By the age of eight or nine, most children will eat almost anything that's offered to them.

By the age of ten children's eating habits are usually firmly established. You will ensure that these are good habits if from the beginning you have offered, and continue to offer, a wide range of nutritious, wholesome foods for meals and for snacks. Children who are satisfied with nutritious foods are less likely to choose high-calorie foods between meals and when they're away from home.

Breakfast is probably the only meal that is a problem for children of this age, but it is the most important meal of the day. There is a long interval between breakfast and lunch, and if breakfast is inadequate or skipped, the time between dinner on one day and lunch the next day is so long that children can become very tired and irritable. This reduces their ability to concentrate and perform well at school, so make sure they get up in time to eat an adequate and unhurried meal.

Schoolchildren

Children's calorie needs are now quite high, as they are still growing and expend a lot of physical and mental energy once they start school. The size of servings varies a lot, depending on the individual's age, size, sex, and level of activity. By the age of ten, many children eat as much as adults, and sometimes more. It is still important to remember never to try to force children to 'clean' their plates or eat a food they don't like. Use the chart on pp. 124–5 as a guide to the amount of food children need from each food group every day.

Devise ways of making breakfast attractive. Change the menus frequently. Whole-grain cereals, milk and

Recommended dietary allowances for energy and protein				
Sex	**Male**		**Female**	
Age	11–14	15–18	11–14	15–18
Weight (kg) (stones)	44.5 7	60.0 9½	44.5 7	54.0 8½
Height (cm) (in)	158 63	172 69	155 62	162 65
Energy (calories)	2800	3000	2400	2100
Protein (grammes) (oz)	44 1.5	54 1.9	44 1.5	48 1.7

fruit make a nutritious meal, but eating exactly the same food every day is boring for anyone, not just children. Provide them with a choice: two cereals, several kinds of fruit, different toppings for pancakes or waffles. Offer foods that are not usually served for breakfast. Cheese or peanut butter sandwiches, cheeseburgers or even nutritious leftovers from dinner can be much more interesting to children than cereal and eggs. Let them prepare one food item themselves.

Let children help you plan the menus a week at a time. Make a chart to put on a kitchen notice board, and get the children to draw pictures to illustrate the food, especially for younger brothers and sisters who cannot read yet.

When children go to school you can no longer supervise everything they eat. Although you may have taught them good eating habits, they may be tempted by sweets and junk foods they see other children eating. Remember the 80/20 rule and don't worry too much, but make sure that they are not consuming too many sweets, fizzy drinks and salty nibbles.

Adolescence

During adolescence children reach a rate of growth second only to that of infancy. As a result of changes in body composition, nutritional needs change, and are different according to sex. The growth spurt usually begins and ends earlier in girls than in boys, but there is so much variation that it is impossible to predict when it will happen to any individual. Any dietary recommendations, therefore, should be used only as general guidelines.

Parents are the last people to affect teenagers' eating habits. Far and away the greatest influence comes from other adolescents – the peer group. Because adolescents are away from home more than before they have much greater control over their choice of foods. Eating becomes part of their social activity and family meals assume much less importance. As a result, food intake is probably more valuable than at any other time.

A balanced low-calorie diet for adolescents

Breakfast	Calories
1 serving fruit or juice	40
170 g (6 oz) whole-grain ready-to-eat cereal	75
225 ml (8 fl oz) skimmed milk	120
1 slice whole-grain bread	60
1 tsp margarine or butter	45
Total	340

Lunch	Calories
60 g (2 oz) lean meat, cheese or fish	175
2 slices wholewheat bread	120
1 tsp margarine or butter	45
1 serving vegetable or fruit	40
225 ml (8 fl oz) skimmed milk	120
Total	500

Dinner	**Calories**
85 g (3 oz) lean meat, fish, poultry or other protein food	250
1 serving vegetable	40
1 salad	40
1 small potato or 115 g (4 oz) rice or noodles or 1 slice wholewheat bread	80
1 tsp margarine or butter	45
1 serving fruit	40
225 ml (8 fl oz) skimmed milk	120
Total	615
Meals total	1455

Snacks (optional)	**Calories**
1 serving fruit	40
115 g (4 oz) ice cream or 1 small cupcake with icing or 3 small biscuits	125
Total	165
Day's total	1620

Daily food guide

Cereals and grains

Whole-grain breads and cereals, brown rice, wholewheat pasta

	Number of servings	1-serving equivalent
3–5 years	4 or more	½–1 slice bread 1 tbsp cereal × years of age
6–10 years	4 or more	1 slice bread 115–225 g (4–8 oz) cereal
11–18 years	4 or more	1 slice bread 115–225 g (4–8 oz) cereal

Fruits and vegetables

All fruits and vegetables. Be sure to include some dark-green or yellow vegetables for vitamin A and some citrus fruits or other source of vitamin C

	Number of servings	1-serving equivalent
3–5 years	4 or more	1 small fruit or vegetable 60–115 g (2–4 oz)
6–10 years	4 or more	1 medium fruit or vegetable 115–140 g (4–5 oz)
11–18 years	4 or more	1 medium fruit or vegetable 115–225 g (4–8 oz)

Meat, fish and eggs

Lean meats, fish, poultry, eggs, dried peas and beans. 1 egg *or* 115 g (4 oz) peas/beans *or* 2 tbsp peanut butter is equal to 30 g (1 oz) of meat

	Number of servings	1-serving equivalent
3–5 years	2 or more	30–85 g (1–3 oz) meat
6–10 years	2 or more	60–115 g (2–4 oz) meat
11–18 years	2 or more	85–115 g (3–4 oz) meat, fish or poultry

Milk and dairy products

Semi-skimmed and skimmed milk, natural yoghurt, ice cream, cheese and other dairy products

	Number of servings	1-serving equivalent
3–5 years	2–3	115–225 ml (4–8 fl oz) milk
6–10 years	under 9: 2–3 over 9: 3 or more	225 ml (8 fl oz) milk
11–18 years	3 or more	225 ml (8 fl oz) milk

All adolescents are concerned about their body shape and image, but studies have shown that whereas teenage boys very often want to increase their weight, teenage girls want to decrease theirs. As a result many teenage girls try to reduce their calorie intake by excluding nutritious foods such as bread, cereals and meat, and filling up on 'empty' high-calorie snacks and soft drinks. As many as one girl in ten may be trying to control her weight by some means – a few are very unhealthy and others positively dangerous. If any teenager is overweight and wants to go on a diet, make sure that it is a sensible one, such as the one given on pp. 122–3.

Surveys show that eating patterns change and the number of meals eaten varies from one to six. Breakfast and lunch are the meals most often skipped, especially by girls on diets. Patterns often become irregular because of school activities, social demands and part-time jobs. The nutrient intake may be well over what a teenager needs one day and well under the next. But remember that it's not necessary to meet *all* food needs *every* day, as long as you have an adequate intake over a week.

To make sure that your children get an adequate intake, encourage them to eat breakfast by offering non-traditional breakfast foods and keeping a good supply of nutritious foods on hand for snacks. Adolescents are very keen on snacking and there is incontrovertible evidence that they can get all the nutrients they need from healthy snacks. Although some of the foods adults usually malign may not be as lacking in nutrition as you think, they should still be eaten only occasionally rather than forming the main part of the diet. The table on pp. 124–5 shows the amount of food from each group that adolescents need.

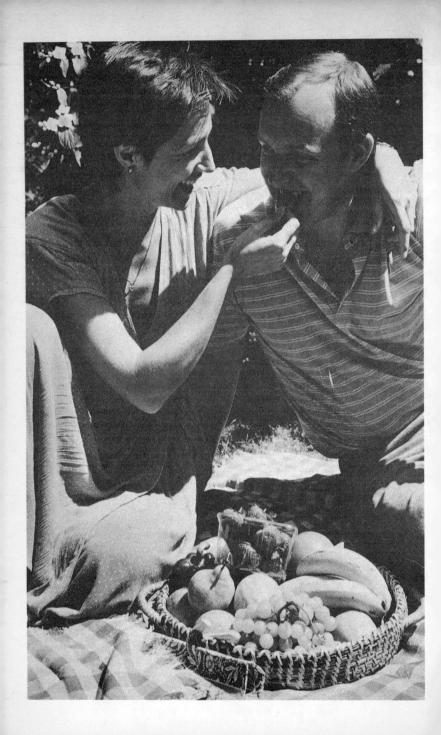

Chapter 5
Serious eating problems

Stress

Stress affects eating adversely, as anyone who's tried to eat before an exam knows. The human body reacts to physical or mental stress by preparing to cope with it or run from it – the 'fight-or-flight' reaction. It produces a high level of adrenalin, which increases activity in some parts of the body and decreases it in others. The pupils become larger so that you can see better; the muscles get tense, ready to run; sugar is released from the body's stores to provide energy and the blood is drawn to the muscles, leaving the skin pale. Adrenalin also depresses the level of insulin, the hormone that regulates the blood sugar. As a result, your blood sugar level tends to rise and you feel this as a loss of appetite. Thus you can concentrate on responding to your situation without being distracted by the need or desire to eat.

When the muscles of the stomach and intestines contract under mild stress, you might feel a little excited or have 'butterflies in the stomach'. Under greater stress, the muscle contractions can be much more severe. Then the stomach feels knotted or unpleasantly full, and the smell of food can bring on waves of nausea. If the muscles of the intestine contract very hard, they can go into a spasm, trapping bubbles of air and faeces and causing intermittent pain until the stress is over. When a person is subjected to intense stress, the stomach can go into reverse peristalsis. The contractions that normally empty the stomach into the excretory system move in the opposite direction and push the food up so that it is vomited.

Most of us are subject to stress for relatively short periods. As soon as the stress is removed, the adrenalin level drops, the insulin level rises and you may suddenly feel very hungry. If stress is prolonged, however, the body remains in a state of preparedness. Long-term stress or anxiety can cause persistent nausea and intermittent bouts of abdominal pain, vomiting, constipation or diarrhoea. It disturbs the body's metabolism, which can result in the breakdown of protein and the loss of potassium, vitamin C and calcium. Healthy eating, therefore, is of vital importance when you are under stress. Unfortunately, a few people respond to stress by losing interest in food and eating infrequently, while most people react by over-eating and eating the least healthy foods. It is important to realize that children can suffer from stress in this way too.

There are two patterns of stress-induced eating. In acute stress, which lasts only a short time, the eating is nearly always brief but intense, the food is nearly always very sweet and the person feels better unless guilt supervenes. Prolonged stress, such as waiting for exam results or working very hard to meet a schedule, is usually less intense and the eating takes the form of constant nibbling and snacking. As long as the stress continues, the hand feeds the mouth.

While you're aware that you're over-eating when you're tense or anxious, you're not really prepared to discipline yourself because you're in the middle of an unpleasant situation and your willpower is at a low point. In these circumstances most people simply don't care about eating an extra chocolate bar. They feel they can 'pig their way out' of tense, worrying situations and adopt a pattern of eating as a way to cope with stress.

The solution to these eating problems is not easy, but it's possible. It involves consciously controlling the otherwise automatic responses. During acute stress eat a 'coping' food. A coping food is one that contains substantial amounts of carbohydrate, such as a chocolate bar, ice cream or a cream cake. High-carbohydrate foods promote the manufacture of a chemical called serotonin, which makes you feel calmer and happier, and therefore better able to cope with stress and other problems. Choose a food that you absolutely adore eating, but usually avoid because you know it's not nourishing. A food you fantasize about is a perfect coping food. Decide that you will eat this food only in a crisis.

When that crisis strikes, try to find a quiet, comfortable spot, make a cup of tea or coffee, put your feet up and then enjoy yourself. The coping food won't work effectively if you wolf it down, so eat very slowly. Don't think about anything else, just savour each mouthful as it goes down. This will have the maximum effect in combating your anxiety, worry or depression. If you have the time, wait for several minutes – twenty minutes is ideal – and you will feel calmness spreading over you. The cause of your stress will not have disappeared, but you'll be in a better state to cope with it.

Think of coping food as an edible tranquillizer, much safer and better than tranquillizing pills. It is important to eat only one portion of coping food. It's not a licence for gluttony. If you find you cannot stop after one portion, then you're suffering from stress-induced bingeing (see pp. 138–40) and you should seek help.

The automatic response to chronic mild stress is continuous nibbling. The stress is alleviated not by foods that affect your mood, but by the act of putting something into your mouth over and over again. Research has shown that touching the mouth repeatedly with the fingers can be very soothing, although many people are unaware of doing it. To cope with this kind of stress, nibble high-fibre, low-calorie vegetables like celery, cucumber, radishes, mushrooms, baked potato skins, cauliflower, and so on, so that you can continue the comforting touching of your mouth while consuming only a few calories. You can also eat low-fat, low-calorie, starchy items like unsugared wholewheat cereals and wholewheat bread. Break the nibbling food into small bite-sized portions and eat everything with your fingers; never use cutlery even if it means taking one granule of cereal at a time. If you nibble very small pieces, you can make the food last a long time. You might find sipping through a straw or sucking home-made frozen fruit juice lollipops comforting too.

Of course, it would be better to overcome the stress without over-eating and better still to avoid it altogether. A healthier way of combating stress is to relax, and the exercises below and on pp. 134–5 can help you to relax physically and mentally.

Physical relaxation

1 Find a quiet place and lie on your back in a comfortable position, or if this isn't possible, sit comfortably, then close your eyes.

2 The next part of the drill involves your right hand if you are right-handed or your left hand if you are left-handed. Begin by tensing your right hand for just a moment, and then relaxing it

completely. Tell your hand to feel heavy and warm. Give yourself a few seconds for these feelings to develop. Do the same, in turn, with your right forearm, upper arm, shoulder, foot, lower leg and upper leg. Then do exactly the same thing with the left side of your body. Your hands, arms and legs should feel heavy, relaxed and warm.

3 Next relax the muscles of your hips, and let the relaxation flow up from your abdomen into the chest. Don't try to tense these muscles, just tell them to feel heavy and warm. Wait until you find that your breathing starts to slow down.

4 Now let the relaxation go up into your neck, jaw and the muscles of your face. Pay special attention to the muscles around your eyes and forehead. Get rid of any frowns. Finish the drill by telling your forehead to feel cool.

Practise this drill twice a day if you can, for fifteen to twenty minutes each time. Even a few minutes, as little as three, is better than nothing. The best time to practise is just before meals and an hour or more after meals. Once you have mastered the technique of deep muscle relaxation, you are ready to go on to mental relaxation.

Mental relaxation

Mental relaxation means clearing your mind of any worries or stressful thoughts. This exercise will help you.

1 Just let any thoughts flow through your head.

2 If any thought recurs, stop it by saying 'no' under your breath.

3 With your eyes closed, imagine any calm scene. The most calming is probably a clear blue sky and a calm blue sea, or an object that has no detail. Do try to see the colour blue, because this has been found to be a particularly relaxing colour.

4 Think about your breathing and become aware that it is slow and natural. Concentrate on your breathing, and follow each breath as you inhale and exhale.

5 By now you should be feeling calm and rested. You may find it helpful to repeat a soothing word such as love or peace or calm, or a word with less symbolism such as breath, earth, laugh, or even a calming sound like 'ah'. Think of the word or sound silently in your mind when you are exhaling.

6 Remind yourself to keep the muscles of your face, eyes and forehead relaxed and tell your forehead to feel cool.

Avoiding or managing stress is not easy. There is a plethora of books on the market telling you how to do it. One technique you might try is, in calmer moments, to write down the sort of things that make you feel stressed and then consider ways to prepare yourself for them or manage them. For instance, you might find that you always start to eat as soon as your children come home from school. You might realize that it is because they're very active and make a lot of noise and mess. Perhaps you can arrange for an older child or a neighbour to look after them for just a few hours or to supervise their play so that it does not disturb you; or you might plan after-school activities that will keep your children entertained without disturbing you.

Anorexia nervosa

Anorexia nervosa is a disorder that occurs mainly in adolescent girls and young women, and is characterized by extreme dieting or self-induced starvation. At the least it interferes with normal bodily development and functions, and at worst it is fatal. The causes of anorexia are not yet fully understood, but include fear of sexuality and adult responsibilities, low self-esteem and inferiority.

During puberty a girl's body undergoes dramatic changes: her breasts begin to develop, her hips and abdomen become rounder, she begins to menstruate and becomes aware of sexual feelings. Some girls are unable to cope with these feelings and the responsibilities of adulthood, and wish to withdraw into childhood. Extreme dieting stops menstruation and the development of secondary sexual characteristics, and a girl's body regresses to a pre-adolescent, childlike state.

We know that being overweight is bad for our health, but our society also puts an unhealthy emphasis on being slim. Most adolescent girls are concerned about their appearance and their popularity, which they see as closely linked. Girls who do not have a sense of belonging and who feel inferior to their peers often are convinced that they'll be more popular if they have the 'ideal' slim figure. They can become obsessed with dieting to try to achieve a size and shape that may be impossible given their bone structure and other genetic factors. Their body image becomes distorted, and they see themselves as fat even when they are skeletally thin.

Adolescence is also a time of striving for independence and searching for an identity. Sometimes parents or other adults in authoritative positions are domineering and try to retain complete control of children's lives. This conflict leads some young people to open rebellion while others feel insecure and find subtler ways of exerting control over their own lives. Ceasing to eat is one way of doing this. Girls who limit their consumption of food and lose weight as a result feel a tremendous satisfaction. Here is one area of their lives they have the power to control. The less they eat, the thinner they become, the more control they have and the more secure they feel.

Initially, a girl may be proud of her ability to resist food, to show her self-control, and will make no effort to hide it. However, when the dieting becomes extreme and she is pressurized to eat by her parents, she will usually feign normality and become furtive about her eating habits.

Anorexia can be cured, although it may take a long time. Parents need to be aware that it is a psychological problem, and although force-feeding may save a girl's life in the short term, it doesn't cure the condition. It is essential that the anorexic person recognizes that she is ill and needs help. Parents, teachers and friends will probably not be able to convince her, and it is best to get help from the family doctor or one of the organizations concerned with treating anorexia. When the girl has accepted treatment, her family and friends can help her build up her self-confidence and set herself realistic goals. It's very good for an anorexic to hear over and over again that she is liked and valued for herself.

Bulimia nervosa

Although a separate condition, bulimia is similar to anorexia in many ways. It is characterized by periods of self-induced starvation alternating with bingeing – uncontrollable eating – followed by self-induced vomiting or the use of large doses of laxatives to get rid of the food. Bulimia affects millions of women in the Western world at some time in their lives and may be a reaction to stress or to suppressed feelings of anger or frustration, or may be triggered by a period of extreme dieting.

When a person is starving, she feels tired because her body isn't getting enough fuel, and she feels depressed because her body is producing an insufficient amount of the mood-regulating chemical serotonin. When she allows herself to eat, she feels a sudden burst of energy and euphoria as her body burns the calories and produces a higher level of serotonin; she craves more food to maintain that level. The craving and the eating become uncontrollable and the result is an eating binge. Subsequently she may feel guilty about her eating and worried that she will gain weight, or she may wish to exert control over this area of her life in defiance of parents who have pressurized her into eating. By vomiting or purging herself with laxatives, she feels she is controlling her bingeing, her weight and her life. She might also take excessive exercise to burn up calories and then begin dieting again. It becomes a vicious circle.

Starving, bingeing, vomiting and purging are very dangerous. Starvation leads to mineral and vitamin deficiencies, while in extreme cases bingeing can cause death by bursting the stomach. Chronic vomiting causes mouth ulcers and erosion of the teeth. Repeated use of large quantities of laxatives causes severe abdominal pain and intestinal damage, and depletes the body of its stores of minerals, particularly potassium, which is essential to the health of the heart and kidneys. Many bulimics suffer from acid stomachs and peptic and gastric ulcers.

Bulimics can be cured, but progress is usually slow. Although one should consult a doctor about any serious health problem, the cure rate for bulimia is higher among self-help groups.

Alcoholism

If a person drinks excessive amounts of alcohol regularly, his or her body develops a tolerance, which means that larger and larger amounts are needed to achieve the same effect. At some point the body's functions adapt to the changes caused by the alcohol so that they are then severely disrupted without it; the person has become alcohol-dependent, an alcoholic. Alcoholism has disastrous effects on every aspect of a person's life. It can damage the liver, digestive system, nervous system and brain, and it can cause death. It often leads to depression, violence, unemployment, and rejection by family and friends.

Many people are able to enjoy a few drinks occasionally with no ill effects. They may drink because it relieves tension or, by releasing inhibitions, makes them feel more at ease in a social gathering. The people who develop an alcohol problem often lack self-confidence and self-esteem, and feel inadequate. They may drink to escape loneliness, boredom or responsibilities and problems they feel they can no longer cope with.

Alcoholism and alcohol-related problems are increasing among young women, particularly those under the age of thirty. This is probably because more and more women are following what was formerly considered a man's life, and are subject to the same stresses and strains that has produced alcoholism in men. These women are attaining positions of responsibility in their careers and may also be assuming the burdens of running a home and raising children. Other women may undergo an identity crisis if they have devoted all their adult lives to their family and then are left alone as their children grow up and are no longer dependent on them. In addition, they all are vulnerable to the stresses of major life events, such as separation, divorce, bereavement, and unemployment.

Many people are not aware that they have a drinking problem. If you answer 'yes' to any one of the following questions, you are not in control of your drinking and should seek help now.

---

* When faced with a problem, do you turn to alcohol for relief?
* Are you sometimes unable to meet home or work responsibilities because of your drinking?
* Has someone close to you expressed concern about your drinking?
* Have you ever required medical attention as a result of drinking?
* Have you ever had distressing physical or psychological reactions when you have stopped drinking?

* Have you ever experienced a blackout or total loss of memory while still awake when drinking?
* Have you often failed to keep promises you have made to yourself about controlling or stopping your drinking?

If you want to obtain help, the best place to start is Alcoholics Anonymous. If you don't like their style, they'll put you in touch with other organizations that can give you the kind of help you need. You'll find them listed in your telephone directory, or you can contact the head office: Alcoholics Anonymous, PO Box 514, 11 Redcliffe Gardens, London SW10 9BQ. The Health Education Council, 78 New Oxford Street, London WC1A 1AM, can also direct you to other helpful organizations.

Chapter 6
Special diets

Choices for vegetarians

As they learn about healthy eating, more people are turning to a vegetarian diet. A diet that excludes meat and therefore many processed foods, and places a complementary emphasis on fresh fruit and vegetables, usually has fewer calories, less sugar and saturated fats and more fibre than the usual British diet.

There are three types of vegetarian diet. An ovo-lacto vegetarian diet excludes meat and fish, but allows dairy products and eggs. A lacto-vegetarian diet excludes meat, fish and eggs, but allows dairy products. A pure vegetarian, or vegan, diet excludes all animal products, including dairy foods and animal fats, and foods containing them.

The nutritional quality of any diet depends on the amount of variety, so it's easier for an ovo-lacto vegetarian to have a nutritious diet than it is for a vegan. A vegan also has to eat a great deal more food to take in sufficient calories. Nevertheless, studies confirm that it is possible for all types of vegetarian to obtain the nutrients they require. If you are considering changing to a vegetarian diet, here are some guidelines. Many excellent vegetarian cookery books are available and can help you plan your meals.

Protein sources and food combinations

The obvious consequence of a vegetarian diet is that an adequate amount of protein (see pp. 18–21) has to be derived from foods other than meat and fish. The proteins eaten also have to be complete – that is, they must contain the right balance of amino acids for your body to use in building its own proteins. Consuming a sufficient amount of complete protein is fairly easy if you eat dairy products or eggs, or both. If you are a vegan, however, your major protein sources are pulses, cereals and other vegetables, which each lack certain essential amino acids. Soya beans are a very good protein source, containing almost as many essential amino acids as animal foods. Soya beans are made into soya milk and soya flour. Their protein can also be extracted, textured or spun, and then flavoured to resemble meat.

All vegetarians can be sure of getting complete proteins by eating certain foods together *at the same*

Vegetable protein sources

	Protein content	
	g/100 g	g/oz
Soya flour, low-fat	45.3	12.9
Cheese, hard	26.0	7.4
Peanuts	24.3	6.8
Peanut butter	22.6	6.4
Textured vegetable protein	17.0	4.8
Almonds	16.9	4.8
Cheese, cottage	13.6	3.9
Oatmeal, dry	12.4	3.5
Eggs	12.3	3.5
Brazil nuts	12.0	3.4
Walnuts	10.6	3.0
Bread, wholewheat	8.8	2.5
white	7.8	2.2
Lentils, boiled	7.6	2.2
Cob or hazel nuts	7.6	2.2
Baked beans	5.1	1.4
Peas, boiled	5.0	1.4

| | Protein content | |
	g/100 g	g/oz
Spaghetti or macaroni, boiled	4.2	1.2
Sweetcorn, kernels	4.1	1.2
Soya milk	3.4	1.0
Milk	3.3	0.9
*Rice, boiled	2.2	0.6
Chestnuts	2.0	0.6
Potatoes, boiled	1.4	0.4

*Grains are important too in obtaining vegetable protein.

meal. It's really quite easy; just remember the following combinations:

* Eggs or dairy products + any vegetable protein – for example, cauliflower and cheese sauce, poached eggs on spinach, rice-and-date pudding.
* Cereals + pulses – for example, oats and lentil stew, rice and kidney beans, sweetcorn and bean chowder.
* Pulses + seeds and nuts – for example, bean salad with almonds, hummus (a blend of chick-peas and tahini, or sesame seed paste), tofu and sesame seeds.

Vitamins and minerals

Because milk contains many of the vitamins and
minerals lacking or in short supply in some vegetables,
you can meet these nutritional requirements if you are
a lacto or ovo-lacto vegetarian and your diet includes a
great variety of plant foods.

If you are a vegan, you have to plan your diet very
carefully to make sure you get sufficient amounts of
calcium, iron and vitamins B_{12} and D. Some green
vegetables, including spinach, broccoli, and mustard
greens, contain significant amounts of calcium. Other
sources are okra, white cabbage, turnips, almonds, and
most dried fruits. Some flours may also be fortified with
calcium.

Your body can absorb only a tiny percentage of the
iron in vegetables, so you need to eat a lot of foods that
contain a good amount, such as peas, beans, green leafy
vegetables, and iron-enriched bread and cereals. You
might also need to take an iron supplement, but you
should do this only on your doctor's advice.

Vitamin B_{12} is contained only in foods of animal
origin, but you can get it in specially fortified soya milk
and from nutritional (not baker's, brewer's or live)
yeast. Even so, you will probably need to take tablets of
synthetic vitamin B_{12} to avoid deficiency, which can
lead to anaemia and damage to your central nervous
system.

If you expose your skin to sunlight regularly, you
shouldn't have to worry about getting enough vitamin

D. If this isn't possible, you can get margarine fortified with vitamin D or use a vitamin D supplement.

Guidelines for diabetics

Your body uses the carbohydrates, protein and fat in food to give it energy. When you have diabetes, your body does not produce enough insulin or cannot utilize what it produces to burn up the carbohydrates, particularly the sugars, in your diet. Depending on the type of diabetes you have, you may or may not need to take insulin. All diabetics, however, need to modify their diets to some extent.

If you are overweight – a common problem for diabetics – the first thing you should do is reduce to a healthy weight. If you are within the normal weight range for your height and build, the following dietary guidelines will help you to control your diabetes.

> * Avoid sugar and sugary foods, such as cakes, pastries, sweets, chocolate, jelly, fizzy drinks, ice cream, and canned fruits in heavy syrup (see also p. 96).
> * Limit the amount of fat in your diet, for example by using skimmed milk and skimmed milk products, restricting your intake of sausages, mayonnaise, butter, nuts, crisps and fried foods (see also pp. 47–8).
> * Eat lots of complex carbohydrates and high-fibre

foods, particularly wholewheat bread, cereals and pasta; potatoes; peas, broad beans and lentils; and plenty of fresh fruits (see also p. 46).
* Eat regular meals, spread out over the day. If you take insulin, you must be sure to eat an adequate amount after each injection to avoid insulin shock, and you should never delay or skip a meal.

There are a number of cookery books specifically for diabetics, and you can get more information about diets from your doctor, local health authority or The British Diabetic Association, 10 Queen Anne Street, London W1M 0BD.

Allergy and intolerance: different reactions, different remedies

The body's normal response to a foreign substance is to try to get rid of it. An allergy is when the body attacks a substance that normally is not considered 'foreign', such as a food, usually a protein. The symptoms of an allergic reaction are extremely varied. They include itchy skin, rash, eczema, hives, wheezing, stuffy or runny nose, itchy and runny eyes, headache and stomach cramps. The most serious reactions can produce swelling of the eyes, lips and tongue, so that swallowing can be impaired; restriction of the airways, which causes laboured breathing; profound vomiting and diarrhoea; a rapid fall in blood pressure, resulting in kidney failure and possibly even coma and death.

Foods that people are most often allergic to include milk, cheese, eggs (mainly the whites), pork, fish (particularly shellfish and canned fish), sweetcorn, tomatoes, strawberries, nuts, and wheat. An allergy to a particular food may extend to other foods in the same food family. For example, someone who is allergic to green peppers is likely to be allergic to red peppers, chillies, paprika, cayenne and chilli powder, but not to white or black pepper.

The tendency to allergies is inherited. Food allergies usually start when people are young, but can begin at any age. They can also diminish and even disappear without treatment. The usual way of treating a food allergy is to eliminate the food from the diet. This is easy if the food is a simple one, like strawberries. However, it is much more difficult if you are allergic to a food that is frequently used as an ingredient in preparing other foods, such as milk, eggs or wheat.

A suspected allergy should always be investigated by a specialist (an allergist) – not your general practitioner – before any food is excluded from the diet. This is particularly important in the case of a baby. A bout of vomiting or diarrhoea is not necessarily evidence of an allergy; it could be the symptom of an infection or other disease. Amateur diagnosis can result in unnecessarily denying a child or an adult important nutrients, not recognizing potential related allergies, and mistaking an intolerance for an allergy.

An intolerance to a food is often mistaken for an allergy because it may produce similar symptoms, such as abdominal pain and diarrhoea. An allergy is the body's rejection of a food, but an intolerance is the inability to digest it. Frequently, an intolerance begins at a certain level, and so it may not be necessary to completely eliminate a food from your diet, but just reduce the amount you eat. For example, one of the most common intolerances is to lactose, the sugar in milk. You might be able to eat a bowl of yoghurt, a milk product, with no ill effects, but find that drinking a glass of milk gives you an upset stomach. An allergist will be able to tell you if you or your children are suffering from an intolerance or an allergy, and what you should do about it.

There has been a vogue for attributing hyperactivity in children, aggressive behaviour, poor concentration, and sleeplessness to food allergies and particularly to food additives. The prevalence of reactions to food additives is extremely low, less than one in ten thousand, and although there may be some connection between foods and these behaviour problems, there is very little scientific evidence to support it.

Gluten intolerance

Gluten is a protein found in wheat, rye, barley, oats and some other foods. In some people the lining of the small intestine is sensitive to, and cannot absorb, the gluten; they have a gluten intolerance, also called coeliac disease. This inability to tolerate gluten upsets the absorption of fats, minerals and vitamins. A child with a gluten intolerance may eat an adequate diet but still be undernourished. He will be irritable, lethargic and extremely thin; have a protuberant abdomen; lose his appetite; and have pale, bulky, frothy and foul-smelling faeces that float.

Depending on the severity of the intolerance, it may

Gluten intolerance checklist

	Gluten-free foods	Gluten-containing foods
Milk	Milk – fresh, dried, skimmed Cream – fresh, soured Cheese	Yoghurt Synthetic cream Cheese spreads, processed cheese
Meat	All fresh meat, including bacon, ham, poultry	Any cooked with flour or breadcrumbs Sausage rolls, pies Sausages, proprietary beefburgers Meat paste, pâté Canned meat
Fish	All fresh fish, shellfish Canned fish in oil or water	Any cooked in batter or breadcrumbs Canned fish in sauce Fish fingers, fish cakes
Eggs	Eggs	
Pulses	Dried peas, beans, lentils	

be necessary to follow a gluten-free diet. The table on pp. 154–7 shows that there is a wide range of foods that you will have to avoid, but an equally wide range that you can eat. Use the menus on pp. 158–61 to help you plan gluten-free meals for children or adults.

	Gluten-free foods	Gluten-containing foods
Cereals	Rice, maize (sweetcorn), buckwheat, millet	Wheat, barley, rye
	Sago, tapioca, gluten-free semolina	Semolina
	Oats – porridge oats, oatmeal	
	Gluten-free flour, cornflour, arrowroot, potato flour, soya flour, split pea flour, rice flour	Ordinary flour
	Soya and rice bran	Wheat bran, wheat-germ
		All ordinary bread, crispbread, cakes and biscuits
		Ordinary pasta – macaroni, spaghetti, noodles, ravioli
	Cornflakes and rice breakfast cereals	All other breakfast cereals and muesli
		Baby cereals and infant foods
		Communion wafers

	Gluten-free foods	Gluten-containing foods
Fruit and vegetables	All raw, canned, dried and frozen fruit All fresh, frozen and dried vegetables, including potatoes Canned vegetables in water or brine	Pie fillings, proprietary baby and infant fruits Vegetable dishes including flour Canned vegetables in sauce (e.g., baked beans) Instant potato Potato crisps
Soups		Canned and packet soups
Puddings	Rice, sago, tapioca, gelatin, jelly	Semolina, proprietary sponge or pastry puddings Dessert mixes, ice cream, mousses, pie fillings, canned milk puddings, infant desserts, custard powder, canned custard Cake decorations Cooking chocolate
Fats	Butter, lard, margarine, cooking oil, olive oil, fresh suet	Packet suet
Nuts	Nuts	Dry roasted peanuts Peanut butter

	Gluten-free foods	Gluten-containing foods
Seasonings and sauces	Salt, freshly ground pepper, herbs, pure spices, vinegar	Curry powder, mustard, mixed spices and seasonings, stock cubes, gravy mixes, savoury spreads, sauces, chutneys/pickles, salad dressings
Sugars, preserves and sweets	Jam, marmalade, honey, golden syrup, molasses, black treacle, sugar	Mincemeat, lemon curd, lemon cheese, chocolate and sweets
Raising agents	Yeast, cream of tartar, tartaric acid, bicarbonate of soda	Baking powder
Flavourings	All food flavourings and colourings	Beef essence, chicken essence, milkshake flavourings
Beverages	Tea, coffee, fruit juice, squashes, fizzy drinks	Barley water, cocoa, drinking chocolate, proprietary milk drinks, vending-machine drinks, tomato juice
Alcoholic drinks	All except beer	

Gluten-free family menus

Day 1

Breakfast	Lunch	Dinner
Muesli	Salade niçoise	Cream of pea soup
Yoghurt	Pizza*	Beef casserole
Brown bread*	Fresh fruit	Fruit sorbet

Day 2

Breakfast	Lunch	Dinner
Fresh fruit	Tomato soup	Pasta* salad
Cottage cheese	Fish pie	Old-fashioned
Millet bread*	Fresh fruit	rice pudding

Day 3

Breakfast	Lunch	Dinner
Yoghurt	Kidney bean,	Mackerel pâté
Dried apricot	courgette and	Vegetable curry
purée	mushroom	Raspberry sorbet
Cornbread*	salad	
	Spaghetti* and	
	tomato sauce	
	Fresh fruit	

Day 4

Breakfast	Lunch	Dinner
1 egg	Kedgeree	Onion soup
Freshly squeezed	Fresh fruit	Lentil roast
orange juice		Apple pie*
Banana bran		
bread*		

Day 5

Breakfast	Lunch	Dinner
Cereal*	Cream of celery soup	Stuffed peppers
Tomato juice	Savoury flan*	Lemon chicken with mushrooms
Bran fruit loaf*	Fresh fruit	Pancakes*

Day 6

Breakfast	Lunch	Dinner
Carrot or grape juice	Country pâté	Bacon and lentil soup
Date and walnut loaf*	Potato salad	Steak and kidney pudding*
	Fresh fruit	Fruit salad

Day 7

Breakfast	Lunch	Dinner
Omelette	Minestrone soup	Herrings in oatmeal
Fresh fruit	Stir-fried chicken and bean sprouts	Baked courgettes
Muffins*	Fresh fruit	Baked lemon pudding

* Use gluten-free flour.

Gluten-free menus for children

Day 1

Breakfast	Lunch	Dinner
Brown rice porridge with soaked sultanas and sesame seed meal Milk	Shepherd's pie with minced beef, lamb or chicken Carrots Brussels sprouts	Cottage cheese, apple and finely grated carrot salad on brown rice cakes

Day 2

Breakfast	Lunch	Dinner
Scrambled egg Potato pizza base	Poached fish Vegetables Boiled potato	Brown rice pudding with sultanas (no added sugar)

Day 3

Breakfast	Lunch	Dinner
Basic millet with apricot purée and sunflower seed meal	Slice meat loaf (using brown rice in place of breadcrumbs) Salad	Maize muffins Home-made apple sauce

Day 4

Breakfast	Lunch	Dinner
Fresh fruit salad and natural yoghurt	Lentil and vegetable broth with brown rice in place of barley Puffed brown rice cake and sesame seed spread	Chicken in cheese sauce

Day 5

Breakfast	Lunch	Dinner
Brown rice and ground almond porridge with milk	Grilled fish with banana and lemon juice stuffing	Chicken soup with brown rice and vegetables Savoury egg custard

Day 6

Breakfast	Lunch	Dinner
Potato cheese cake (mashed potato and grated cheese baked or grilled)	Sweet and sour liver Seasonal salad Jacket potato	Fish soup with rice or potato noodles and vegetables, served as a meal in a bowl with not too much broth

Day 7

Breakfast	Lunch	Dinner
Puffed brown rice, puffed millet or puffed corn cereal with toasted seed meal and raisins	Sardines Cup of clear soup	Big bean stew with millet balls (cook millet and bind with egg, roll in sesame seed meal and bake on top of casserole)

Nearly all recipes can be adapted to contain no gluten. For example, you can use flour made from millet, maize, potato, soya bean and chick peas instead

of from wheat. There are also many gluten-free manufactured products. If you find it difficult to separate
your gluten-free cooking from the food for the rest of
the family, prepare all your main dishes using gluten-
free products. The rest of the family can eat foods
containing gluten as accompaniments.

If you are eating in a restaurant, stick to fresh fruits
and plain meat or fish dishes without sauces. Don't eat
fried potatoes because they may have been cooked
in the same oil as battered or breaded foods and so
contain traces of gluten. When you are travelling or on
holiday, take gluten-free bread, biscuits and cereals
with you.

Feeding the sick and convalescent

A person who is ill often does not feel like eating, and
should not have any solid food if he has been vomiting
or has abdominal pain or diarrhoea. Diarrhoea and
vomiting are more serious in children than in adults. If
not properly treated, both conditions can quickly lead
to dehydration, especially in a young baby or a child
who is slight or thin. If the child has a very mild case of
diarrhoea or has vomited only a couple of times
but otherwise seems generally well and lively, simply
make sure he has plenty to drink and keep an eye on
him. Call the doctor if the symptoms persist for
twenty-four hours, if the child seems unwell, or if
diarrhoea is accompanied by vomiting, abdominal
pain and fever.

Depending on the cause and perhaps the severity of the individual's illness, or if he is recuperating from surgery, the doctor might prescribe a specific diet, which you must follow. In the absence of such a special diet, use the information here to guide you.

Although he may not want, or should not have, any solid food, a sick person needs to consume plenty of fluids to replace the moisture he loses through fever and other symptoms. Try to get him to sip a glass of water or other liquid throughout the hour every hour. If the illness has upset his digestion, do not give him milk or milk products, as they have a laxative effect. Also avoid kaolin and pectin preparations, which don't taste nice and can cause vomiting. Otherwise, let him drink whatever he likes and as much as he can. You might have to entice a sick child to drink as much as he needs, so here are some tips for making drinks more interesting.

* Use a straw, especially an interesting curly one.
* Encourage his thirst by giving him a plain salted biscuit or a lollipop to suck.
* Offer him a variety of drinks, including tea, fresh or canned fruit juices diluted with water, and sweet drinks with the fizz removed (a teaspoon of warm water or sugar will remove the carbonation). While sweet drinks should ordinarily be avoided, they're all right when drinking becomes the priority.

* Put a small container of little ice cubes by the bedside and encourage him to suck them.
* Put a picture of a ship or cartoon character on his favourite glass or let him use a glass normally reserved for grown-ups.
* Serve his drinks in a tiny glass; it makes the quantity look easier to finish and it's more fun.
* Children under seven or eight often like to sip fluids from a spoon, and using a long-handled spoon may make it seem more like a game.

How a person eats is as important as what he eats. A convalescent, or a sick person who is allowed solid foods, should eat small meals frequently. It is essential that the patient does not eat too much or too quickly, as this can interfere with his digestion.

Because he is eating small amounts, choose foods that supply the most nutrition for their weight or volume. Ask the patient what he would like and don't insist that he eats any particular food if he doesn't want to, even if it usually is his favourite item. As the patient continues to get better, vary the diet as much as possible, but avoid all rich foods, fatty foods, sauces, cakes, pastries and sweets.

The first solid foods someone, particularly a child, recovering from a gastro-intestinal illness might find acceptable are small amounts of raw carrot, banana, peeled apple or apple sauce. Soon afterwards, he should be able to eat a regular diet of bland foods that do not require digesting, such as scrambled eggs, soufflés, omelettes, soups, puréed vegetables and puréed fruits.

If the patient did not have a gastro-intestinal illness, milk and milk products, which are rich in proteins, should form a large part of his diet. He should try to consume about 500 millilitres (1 pt) of skimmed milk a day in drinks, soups and custard, or in the form of ice cream, yoghurt or cheese.

During the convalescent period eggs can be used as the main source of protein, especially if dairy products are being avoided. They can be served poached, boiled or scrambled, or as an ingredient in other dishes. Supplementary sources of protein are poultry, fish, shellfish and meat. Liver is an excellent source of vitamins and minerals, and can be grilled, baked or gently sautéd.

Fruit and vegetables are, of course, part of any healthy diet. Some fresh fruit should be eaten every day. Citrus fruits, which contain vitamin C, are particularly important during recuperation. Potatoes, cabbage and carrots are also good sources of vitamin C. Cabbage and carrots can be served raw or cooked, and potatoes can be steamed, boiled, mashed or baked. Steamed or rapidly boiled green leafy vegetables such as spinach, broccoli, kale and sprouts can be served with a light dressing of lemon juice or oil and vinegar. Use fresh vegetables whenever possible; otherwise, frozen vegetables are preferable to canned.

To ensure a well-balanced diet serve whole-grain bread and cereals, and add wheat-germ to breakfast cereals. Include some fats in the form of avocado, salad dressing, peanut butter, or tahini dip.

Do not worry if a person does not eat much for a day or two; as his health gradually improves, so will his appetite.

Not eating for two: pregnant women and nursing mothers

If you are following a healthy, well-balanced diet, as explained in the preceding chapters, you will have to make only minor adjustments to accommodate your increased nutritional needs when you are pregnant. It is essential that you do not smoke during pregnancy, and most doctors recommend that you do not drink alcohol.

If possible, make sure you are the right weight for your size before you conceive; you should never try to lose weight when you are pregnant. And while it's normal to eat more during pregnancy, it's not an excuse for over-eating. Your doctor will advise you on your diet and how much weight you should gain, taking into account your current weight, your medical history, whether you have a single or multiple pregnancy, and whether you are an adolescent and therefore still growing yourself. Generally, your energy requirements increase about 15 per cent, which means you need more calories: about 150 more a day in the first three months (a trimester), 300 a day in the second trimester, and 400–450 more in the last trimester.

While your appetite is increasing, your digestive

system is slowing down, and during the last trimester the baby is pushing against your stomach. For your comfort as well as your digestion it is important not to overload the stomach, so try to eat a greater number of smaller meals than usual, say five or six a day instead of three.

For healthy foetal development, your daily diet needs to contain more protein, calcium, phosphorus, iodine, iron, and vitamins A, B, C and D. It can be difficult to get enough iron from the diet alone, so most doctors prescribe iron supplements. Here are the main nutrients you get from the different food groups (see also pp. 55–6).

---

* Milk and dairy products: a high percentage of the protein, most of the calcium and phosphorus, and all of the vitamin D.
* Meat, fish and poultry: a lot of protein, B vitamins and some iron.
* Vegetables, potatoes and citrus fruits: some protein and large quantities of vitamin C; vegetables are also an excellent source of vitamin A.
* Grains and cereals: iron and B vitamins, and smaller amounts of protein, calcium and phosphorus.

Your body requires a lot of liquid now too. In addition to drinking about 1 litre (2 pt) of milk a day, you should try to drink about 1.5 litres (3 pt) of other liquids while you are pregnant, and 2 litres (4 pt) when you are breast-feeding. Avoid fizzy drinks and cut back on tea and coffee; they all contain caffeine, which may not be good for the foetus. When tea is drunk with a meal, the tannic acid it contains can prevent the body from absorbing the iron in the food.

Fresh, unprocessed foods have the highest nutritional value, while foods with added chemical preservatives, colourings and flavourings might be harmful. Therefore buy fresh fruits and vegetables, and eat them raw as often as possible. Do not eat any food that is stale or has mould on it. Cutting off the mould does not always remove the toxins, which may have penetrated deeper and are not destroyed by cooking. Also avoid canned, frozen and packet convenience foods; processed meats, such as sausages and commercial pâtés; products made with refined flour; bottled sauces and pickles; and high-calorie snacks such as crisps, biscuits and sweets.

Eating well in old age

As you get older you should continue to eat a varied and well-balanced diet that provides all the essential nutrients. However, you are probably less active than when you were younger, so you need less food. Your digestive system also slows down, so you will be more comfortable if you eat smaller meals and more snacks. Carbohydrates in the form of fresh fruit and vegetables, potatoes, and whole-grain breads and cereals are easy to digest and very nutritious. Eat plenty of calcium-rich foods (see p. 31). Warm foods and beverages are easier to digest than cold ones and as you also need plenty of liquids every day, you might find that soups and stews are tasty ways to fulfil several requirements.

Some people become absent-minded as they get older and may neglect their diet. If this is your problem, devise ways to overcome it. For example, impose set mealtimes on yourself; plan all your meals and snacks a day at a time and put the menus on the kitchen notice board; have at least one meal or snack a day with a friend, neighbour, or member of the family.

Remember, it is never too late to start a healthy diet. Be sure to set yourself realistic goals and adapt to them gradually. It also helps to remember that you learned your old food preferences, so you can unlearn them and learn new ones. And, of course, you don't have to give up any food entirely. Tell your family and friends what you are doing and they will support you.

Slimming diets

It is unhealthy to be overweight, but most slimming diets don't work in the long term. They fail because they often depend on strict food restriction or exclusion and do not teach you new eating habits, which is what you need to maintain your weight loss when you finish the diet. Extreme, or 'crash', diets, and particularly those that restrict the variety of foods you may eat, are bad for you because they can deprive you of essential nutrients. The only slimming diet that works is one that is easy enough and palatable enough to continue for the rest of your life – and that means a balanced, healthy diet. If you are overweight, following a diet based on the principles given on pp. 55–6 will help you to lose fat, not just weight, and to maintain your new shape.

It's unlikely, however, that everyone will suddenly ignore slimming diets, and to be realistic about your probable weight loss you need to know how your body will respond to them.

The first week can be quite a shock to the body and it's not uncommon to lose as much as 3 kilogrammes (7 lb) even on a fairly generous diet. Don't be fooled into thinking that all of this is fat; a lot of it is glycogen, which has been stored in the liver and muscles, and the water associated with it. After the initial encouraging drop, weight loss settles down to a rather boring 0.5 – 1 kilogramme (1–2 lb) a week, depending on how much you used to eat. For example, if you usually ate 2500 calories a day, a diet of 1500 calories creates an energy deficiency of 1000 calories a day. That's 7000 calories a week, which is equivalent to about 1 kilogramme (2 lb) of body fat.

A diet of 800 calories or less a day is dangerous. No matter how desperately you want to lose weight or what promises a slimming product or programme makes, you should not follow such a diet without your doctor's advice and supervision. If your body is consistently given fewer calories than it needs for healthy living, it adjusts its metabolism so that it functions at a much lower level. After the initial loss, you will soon fail to lose weight. The temptation is to eat even less, and the body responds by adjusting its metabolism to an even lower rate. You become weak, lethargic and your health is seriously endangered.

Never try to lose weight by skipping meals. In fact, dividing your daily food into six small meals can help you slim. Each time you eat, your metabolism temporarily increases and burns off a little more energy than the simple digestion of the food requires. Exercise also increases metabolism and, contrary to popular belief, doesn't increase your appetite (see pp. 196–7).

In choosing a slimming diet, bear in mind that you are choosing a new pattern of eating. Ask the following questions.

---

* Is the diet flexible? Any good diet must be, as few people lead lives so well-organized that they can stick rigidly to restricted menus for any length of time.
* Is the diet too strict? If you have a job, run a home or are active in any way, you cannot, and should not try to, exist on much less than 1200 calories a day. Most slimmers lose quite well on 1500 a day.
* Are the permitted foods acceptable? A diet that suggests eating a lot of something you do not like or rarely eat is bound to fail.
* Does the diet allow a few small indulgences? The majority of people adhere to a diet more easily if it

allows them a treat now and then (see pages
173–4).
* Will the diet fit in with the family meals? No diet
will last if it involves preparing food entirely
different from that eaten by the rest of the family.

Weight-gaining diet

If you are underweight, it can be very difficult to overeat
to gain weight. Even if you eat two to three times as
many calories as usual, you will probably gain only a
little weight, burning off a lot of the excess calories as
heat instead of storing it as body fat. As soon as your
food consumption returns to your normal level, you are
likely to lose quickly any weight you gained. However,
consistent and serious over-eating can result in weight
gain – just look at all the fat people. You're going to have
to make a big effort, but if you want to gain weight, here
are a few guidelines.

* Maintain the normal nutritional balance of a
healthy diet. Use the food-group system as your
guide (see pp. 55–6).
* Do not eat more of only the foods you have
thought of as fattening; more meat, milk and
bread are as valuable in energy and they're better
for you.
* Do not be tempted to buy products claiming to

> promote weight gain in specific parts of the body;
> there is no scientific evidence that this is
> possible.
> * Exercise may improve body shape by building
>   and toning muscles, but it can also increase your
>   energy output. While you should take some
>   exercise to keep fit, don't overdo it.

If you fail to make or maintain a significant weight gain,
do not be too disappointed. You may be at the optimum
weight for your body and you might do more harm than
good by attempting to change. If you are worried about
your weight, talk to your doctor.

Maintaining momentum

It's not easy to stick to a restricted diet of any kind.
There are always temptations to deviate. If you want to
avoid the major pitfalls, remember the following
points.

> * When eating socially, don't fall into the trap of
>   feeling that you owe it to your hostess to eat more
>   than you strictly should or to sample any food
>   that could endanger your health. Do not be
>   embarrassed to explain that you have an allergy
>   or an illness that prevents you from eating a
>   particular food – though don't go on at length

about it! If you are on a calorie-restricted diet, allow yourself a little treat when eating out.

* Guard against losing enthusiasm. It may help to make a contract with yourself or with your family to stick to the diet. If you're attempting to change your basic habits, reward yourself for every step of progress with a small but spoiling purchase or an outing. Take the time to feel good about yourself.

* Your diet may be upset and your morale may flag if your life is interrupted by accidents, illness, domestic problems, difficulties at work, extensive travel and so on. Be flexible. Reset your goals realistically, and don't regard the lapse as a failure.

* Your appetite may be stimulated without warning by the sight of a box of chocolates or the aroma of cooking. Don't allow yourself to succumb in the first few minutes: take a little time to decide whether a treat is appropriate or whether you should try to suppress the craving (see pp. 66–7).

Chapter 7
Practical advice

Eating a healthy diet can save you money. You will spend less on meat, particularly expensive red meat, and on convenience foods. Remember, it is processed, refined and precooked foods that are the least healthy and usually the most expensive. This means, for example, that whole-grain cereals are cheaper than the refined, sugared varieties, and fresh fruits and vegetables in season are cheaper than their canned or commercially frozen equivalents. If you have a deep freeze, you can buy foods in bulk and freeze them for use throughout the year.

Although whole-grain bread and pasta might be more expensive than their white-flour counterparts, they are more filling and more nutritious. That means they are better value for money. The chart on pp. 179–81 shows you which foods are nutritional value for money.

Planning and budgeting

Spending a little time once a week planning all your meals for the week will help you to save money and time. It saves you money because you buy what you need; no food is bought on impulse and later thrown away because you didn't get round to using it. It saves you time because you don't have to spend time before each meal trying to figure out what you are going to prepare and if you have all the ingredients. Because the menu is planned and published – I suggest you pin it up in the kitchen where everyone can see it – other members of the family who get home before you can start preparing the food. The whole family should understand, especially if you have a job outside the home, that it takes teamwork to get a meal ready.

Make it clear that menus are not negotiable. If anyone doesn't want to eat what you have on the menu, then he can go without or prepare something for himself. This is less likely to happen if you involve children in planning the meals. In either case, make a rule that anybody who eats at home, particularly in the evening, does so with the family. Remember, this is probably the main opportunity for the entire family to be together, and it also means that you won't suddenly discover that the food you've planned to use has been devoured, leaving you with a gap in your menu and your budget.

Value for money

	More nutrition for your money	Less nutrition for your money
Meat	Poultry: chicken, turkey Game: pheasant, pigeon, partridge, rabbit, venison Liver and other offal Home-made burgers and meat products from lean minced steak or other meat Low-fat sausages	Pork, beef, lamb Meat pies and pasties Luncheon meat Manufactured burgers, meat pâtés, spreads and speciality sausages Standard sausages and sausage-meat
Fish	Plain frozen fish (no additives) Home-made fish fingers and fish cakes Wet fish, canned tuna, sardines and mackerel	Fish frozen with polyphosphates or in sauces Manufactured fish fingers and other fish in batter Canned fish in sauces and canned shellfish
Bread and cereals	Breads: wholemeal, wheat-germ, granary, mixed-grain, sprouted-seed, pumpernickel and rye Sugar-free breakfast cereals Porridge	White bread and rolls Croissants and other sweetened breads Breakfast cereals containing sugar, salt and food colouring Instant hot cereals

	More nutrition for your money	**Less nutrition for your money**
Fats	Soft vegetable margarines high in polyunsaturates Unsalted butter Polyunsaturated vegetable oils, e.g. sunflower, safflower, corn, olive Home-made salad dressings, e.g. French dressing, vinaigrette	Hard and soft margarines low in polyunsaturates, dairy spreads, low-fat spreads Salted butter Dripping, lard, suet, blended unspecified cooking oils Bottled or other ready-made salad dressings
Vegetables	Fresh fruit and vegetables in season Fruit canned in its own juice Vegetables canned without added salt or sugar Plain frozen vegetables Fresh potatoes	Bruised and over-ripe fruit and vegetables Fruit canned in syrup Vegetables canned with salt and/or sugar Frozen vegetables in sauces Frozen chips, potato waffles, other potato products in batter
Drinks	Milk – see above Fruit juices, both fresh and made from concentrates Naturally carbonated fruit juices and mineral water with added juice	Milk – see above Fruit-flavoured drinks and squash Fizzy drinks with added sugar or artificial sweeteners, colours and flavours

	More nutrition for your money	Less nutrition for your money
Dairy produce	Mature and farmhouse cheeses	Mild cheeses, processed cheeses and cheese slices
	Edam, Gouda and reduced-fat hard cheeses	Blue cheeses and some flavoured cheeses
	Unsweetened and natural yoghurt, low-fat yoghurt	Full-fat yoghurt
	Real fruit yoghurt	Fruit-flavoured yoghurt
	Skimmed and semi-skimmed milk	Full-fat milk and milk with extra fat
	Dried skimmed milk	Dried milk with added fats

Food labels

Reading food labels is a crucial part of economic shopping and a healthful diet. It may seem a bit of an effort at first, but you'll soon get to know the kinds of foods that have large amounts of ingredients you don't want – sugar, fat, salt, artificial colourings – and those that have the ingredients you do want, such as whole grains and fibre. Sometimes you find a food you thought was wholesome has large amounts of an undesirable ingredient. Then there's a feeling of triumph when you realize that simply by excluding it you raise the standard of your family's eating very quickly.

Look at the first ingredient on the label. Manufacturers don't have to put the weight of ingredients on the label, but by law they have to list them in order of weight. No food can be very nutritious if water, salt, fat, or sugar is the first ingredient. If it is the second, third or fourth ingredient, you can give the product your personal rating of usefulness in the family diet, but try not to include too many such items.

There is such a variety of bread available that it is easy to get confused, particularly as the labels don't always give the guidance you need. Unwrapped bread is, of course, exempt from the labelling laws, but the bakery must be able to describe the type accurately. There is no doubt that the most nutritious bread is wholemeal; any bread labelled or called wholemeal has to be made from 100 per cent whole-grain flour.

Bread labelled or called 'brown' is not wholemeal; it is made with only 50 per cent of the whole grain. As the wheat-germ is not always included in brown flour, the bread might be low on vitamins as well as fibre. Granary is a registered trade name for a particular type of flour and the bread made from it. Granary bread is made with a wheatmeal (but not *wholemeal*) flour to which malted wheat grains are added. However, the word 'granary' is used very loosely and often applied to other breads.

High-fibre white bread is made with refined flour to which a little pea-plant fibre has been added. It does not have the same nutritional value as wholemeal bread.

Tips for busy mothers

* Always make a list before you go shopping. It makes your shopping faster and you won't forget anything you need or buy anything you don't need.
* If you have a car, you can save time and energy by doing all your shopping once a week. However, if you don't have a car, it is better to shop more often than to try to carry heavy loads.
* If you shop once a week, you're likely to go to a large, busy supermarket. To make your job easier and to avoid stress, ask for someone to help you pack your groceries and to load them in your car.
* If you have a young baby, try to get someone to look after him while you go to the supermarket. It is best not to take him with you to a crowded shop where germs are easily spread.
* Arrange your larder or kitchen cupboards so that all the members of the family know where everything is kept. For example, keep all the breakfast cereals together on one shelf, all the canned goods on another, and so on. When you bring home a load of groceries everyone present can help you put them away and in your absence find food to prepare for themselves.
* Give children a list of chores to do each day. Post the list and make it clear that they have the responsibility to help run the house. Children

like to help and are good at reminding each other what needs to be done.

* From the time they are very young, train your children to help you in the kitchen. For example, they can fetch items from the refrigerator or larder, bring your dishes or carry them to the sink, and so on. Children love to help with the cooking and it is a good opportunity to teach them about healthy eating.

* Have a system of rewards for jobs well done. It can be something as simple as a star or a substantial treat, like going to the cinema, for a really big job.

* Involve your children in planning the week's menus and choosing foods. For example, let them help decide which fruits they would like for snacks and which vegetables for main meals, and show them how much cheaper fresh foods are than canned or frozen ones. Let them choose a cheese they really like and pick their favourite real-fruit yoghurts. You know they'll eat foods they've chosen themselves.

Making the most of your freezer

A freezer preserves perishable foodstuffs and prepared dishes with little loss of flavour, appearance or nourishment. Here are ways it can help you to maintain a healthy diet cheaply and to save time and energy.

* It's essential to label all frozen foods with the date of freezing and the name of the food or list of main ingredients in a prepared dish.
* If you defrost a raw food, you can freeze it after cooking; otherwise you must never refreeze thawed food.
* If you have a young baby who is eating only tiny amounts, freeze puréed fruits and vegetables in ice-cube trays and defrost one or two cubes as you need them. As the baby gets older, you can freeze meal-size portions of stews and casseroles in small containers.
* If you have a job outside the home and don't have time to cook every evening, spend half a day at the weekend cooking and freezing meals for use during the next few weeks. For example, you can make large quantities of three different items, such as stews, casseroles or pasta sauces, and freeze them in meal-size portions. Then you could have three meals every week for three weeks that need only to be defrosted.
* Most seasonings and flavourings intensify during storage, so use less than usual when you plan to freeze a dish.
* Liquids and semi-liquids become thicker; you can dilute them before you freeze them or after you defrost them.
* Soups, purées and stews defrost more quickly than other foods.

* Small quantities freeze better and defrost more quickly than large ones. For convenience freeze most foods in family-size portions, and keep a few larger portions for when you have to entertain unexpectedly.

* You can use a microwave to defrost frozen foods quickly; otherwise always allow frozen foods to defrost at room temperature – do not try to speed the process by immersion in hot water.

* Thoroughly reheat any dish containing meat, poultry or fish. Beat the mixture well if ingredients begin to separate during reheating.

* Buy fresh fruit and vegetables in bulk when they are in season and at their cheapest. Get acquainted with wholesale markets, where foods that won't keep well over the weekend can be obtained at bargain prices late on Saturday morning. Choose the best quality produce, buy it early in the morning, and prepare it for freezing immediately to prevent vitamin loss.

* If you grow your own fruits and vegetables, gather them at *dusk* after a sunny day, when the vitamin content is at its highest. Prepare and freeze them immediately.

* Consult a freezer guide on how to prepare fresh foods for freezing. Generally, you should wash all food immediately, but don't soak it. Steam peaches and tomatoes to loosen their skins, and blanch fruits that discolour easily, like apricots,

and all vegetables to retain the maximum nutritional value. If possible, chill raw food before cutting it, and cut all food so that it packs solidly.

Things you can do for yourself

It's worth using even the smallest garden to grow vegetables. No vegetables you buy taste as good as freshly picked ones, and when you grow your own, you can be certain that they are free of artificial fertilizers and pesticides. As well as being healthier and more delicious, they're more convenient. If your garden produces more than the family can eat, you can always freeze the excess (see above).

One reason why I was keen to have a garden was that I wanted my children to grow up knowing that fruits and vegetables don't spring up in supermarkets. I wanted them to have the pleasure of watching something they had planted grow and of monitoring the seasons by our garden produce. If you have a garden, give your children a little patch; help them to pick and eat their produce. It'll be a source of great pride. Of course, not everyone has a garden, but you can grow some vegetables – for example, tomatoes, lettuces, radishes, herbs – in window boxes.

Making jam
Like many women, I used to think that old-fashioned tasks like making jam, bottling fruit, preparing pickles

and chutneys and baking bread were shrouded in mystery and extremely difficult. But common sense suggests that such tasks can't be hard because in the old days everyone had to undertake them, and most people made a pretty good job of them. In fact, they are easy and can be very enjoyable. The smell of newly baked buns and loaves and the sight of rows of jamjars and bottled fruit, shining like jewels, give enormous pleasure.

There are only three ingredients in jam: fruit, sugar and water. You need hardly any water with the very soft fruits; if you are using a hard fruit, the recipe will tell you how much water to add.

First boil the fruit until it is soft and cooked through. Then dissolve the sugar in the fruit juice and bring the jam to a boil. Now you proceed according to one of two methods – slow or fast. With the slow method you boil the fruit until it is very soft; it loses its shape but releases its pectin, which makes the jam set easily. With the fast method you boil the fruit for only a few minutes; it stays whole and pleasant to chew, but because it does not release its pectin, you have to add that.

Next you test the jam by dropping a tiny amount into a cold saucer to see if it forms a skin. If it does, remove the jam from the heat, allow it to cool and pour it into jars that you have sterilized by putting them in the oven for about 45 minutes at a moderate heat. If the drop of jam does not form a skin, boil the mixture for a little longer, then test again.

Home-made jam will last a long time. With some

pride you can reach for a jar of your own jam three years after you've made it, and it will still be in mint condition. One of the prettiest features of home-made jam can be its labelling. Make your own labels, and date and sign them.

Once you've discovered how easy it is to make jam, consult some of the many cookery books on the market for recipes for preserves, bottled fruit, pickles and chutney. All make marvellous presents, so always reserve a few jars for giving away.

Baking bread

Do try baking your own bread. It tastes better; you know exactly what it contains; you can make it into all sorts of shapes and sizes to attract the children; and the smell in the kitchen is wonderful. And baking bread will not take up much of your time – if you start baking at 9.30 a.m., you can have beautiful bread by midday.

Like jam-making, baking requires only a few ingredients:

* flour, preferably wholemeal or a mixture of strong white and wholemeal, though you can ring the changes with different wholemeal flours and by adding exciting ingredients such as chopped onion, grated garlic, cheese and dried or fresh fruit
* a pinch of salt

* yeast – fresh yeast is best, but you can get very good results with dry yeast
* sugar
* warm water or skimmed milk mixed with water; you can vary the texture of your bread by mixing different proportions of milk and water
* a little vegetable oil, preferably sunflower or safflower, and a few drops of sesame oil for a nutty flavour.

You will have to turn to a good cookery book for exact quantities and baking times for different types of bread, but my outline method below will show you how easy it is to produce delicious, wholesome loaves and buns.

The first step is to put the flour into a warm dish, preferably a metal one. Sprinkle the salt on the flour and mix well (use salt sparingly – too much salt will stop the dough from rising).

Make a deep well in the flour. Into it pour a yeast mixture made from the yeast, the sugar and the hand-hot water, which you have left in a warm place until the yeast has risen to the top and the surface is covered with bubbles. This usually takes about 15 or 20 minutes. Stir all the ingredients very thoroughly, adding the oil little by little as you stir.

Now knead the dough. One of the secrets of good bread is good kneading. It's a job that requires a lot of elbow grease unless you do as I've done, which is to invest in a dough hook for my electric mixer – it does all the hard work for me. If you are using a dough hook, I recommend that you knead for at least three or four minutes, stopping now and again to judge the consistency of the dough. Don't knead for too long, though, or the dough will become tough and inelastic.

After the first kneading, take the dough out of the bowl and place it in a dish, cover it with a cloth and stand it in a warm part of the kitchen. Look at it every ten minutes; after half an hour it should be well risen. At this point, knead it again.

Choose baking tins that are an appropriate size for loaves, baps or buns and grease them thoroughly. Divide the dough, roughly shape it and place it in the tins, cover it with a cloth and allow to rise again for 15–20 minutes. When the dough has risen fully, brush the top very lightly with egg wash and put the tins into a pre-heated oven. You will get the best results if your oven is on the hot side, so that the dough bakes quite quickly and therefore retains moisture but acquires a crisp crust. This rarely takes longer than 25–30 minutes for loaves and 15–20 minutes for buns.

Chapter 8
Exercise

In the last decade or so the idea that strenuous exercise can postpone death has grown into a kind of religion whose vestments are leotards and tracksuits, trainers and sweatbands. Sports shops now stock so many different kinds of shoes that you wonder how you ever got by on just a pair of plimsolls. Lissom ladies of television and film fame promote their personal exercise programmes in books and on videos and tape cassettes, and keep fit classes abound. Sceptics and critics, however, point to the number of injuries sustained by joggers and marathon runners and the damage done to women pushed into excessive aerobic exercise by inexperienced teachers. A balanced view is necessary and here's my advice.

To be healthy and fit you need to exercise as well as eat the right foods. Exercise keeps you agile and strong, and helps to improve the efficiency of your heart, lungs and other vital organs. It helps to counteract fatigue and stress, and even helps you to sleep. Exercise builds stamina, so the more you do, the more you will be able to do. Although exercise should be part of your way of life and that of your children from the earliest age, it's never too late to start.

But do be careful – if you've had a sedentary lifestyle until now, don't suddenly take strenuous exercise. First, consult your doctor to see how fit you are, particularly if you are overweight, have recently been ill or had surgery, or have a history of asthma or bronchitis, back pain, arthritis, or high blood pressure. Ask his advice on what kind and how much exercise you should take. If you decide to go to a keep fit or aerobics class, make sure the instructor is qualified to teach, not just an enthusiastic amateur.

Remember that good exercise is not painful. Muscles need to be stretched and conditioned, but they should never be made to burn or ache. To prevent injury, you need to warm up before, and cool down after, you exercise. Stop exercising immediately if you feel breathless or dizzy, or have any pain.

What kind of exercise?

You don't need excessive, vigorous exercise to start on the road to fitness. A brisk walk every day and using stairs instead of lifts is a good beginning. If you want to jog, make sure you have the right kind of shoes for the surface you will run on, and read the tips on pp. 197–8.

Swimming is probably the best all-round exercise for everyone. It exercises all the muscles in the body, is good for the joints, and can be done at any pace you like. Because you are supported by the water and are working against water resistance instead of gravity, you seem to have to make less effort and you have less risk of injury.

A slow game of tennis when you're unfit can be just as enjoyable as a fast game when you're fit. If you play tennis two or three times a week for about six weeks, you'll probably find that you can run round the court and play harder than you thought you ever would. Badminton and squash are other popular games.

Find out what other activities are offered at your community centre or local sports centre, or in evening classes. You might find an old favourite – perhaps netball or hockey – or you might want to try something you've never done before, such as weight-training or yoga.

Tips for walking

In the beginning

* Walk on level ground, avoiding hills.
* Don't walk into the wind. It greatly increases your work load. If you suffer from heart disease, you may be able to walk comfortably for one or

---

two miles with the wind behind you, but you might get severe angina if you walk facing the wind.
* Walk at your natural pace and within your ability to breathe easily.

Aim to

* Gradually increase the pace at which you walk, but always keep within your ability to breathe easily. You should be able to hold a conversation while you are walking.
* Gradually increase the distance you walk.
* Work at your walking until you can walk about three miles without stopping in 45–55 minutes, then you are ready to begin a walking/jogging programme.

Walking/jogging

* Start by walking briskly for about 5 minutes, then jog for 3 minutes, walk for another 5 minutes or until you feel ready to jog again.
* Repeat this cycle for about 20 minutes.
* Do it at least every other day, but not more than five days a week.
* When you can manage this programme comfortably, you are ready to start a jogging programme.

Tips for jogging

Technique

* Run with your arms bent at the elbows and your wrists and fingers held loosely. Your hands should just about scratch your abdomen as you run.
* Don't lean forward. Keep your back straight, your head up and your shoulders relaxed. If you feel a bit stiff, shake your arms to ease your shoulders. Look about 5.6 metres (15–20 feet) in front of you, not down at your feet.
* Keep your stride fairly short.
* When you land, always take the weight on the heel of your foot, roll forward on to the ball and push off. Don't try to run on your toes, as that will strain your calf muscles.
* Breathe regularly and deeply, pushing your abdomen out as you inhale and making a noise to emphasize exhaling. Never hold your breath.

In the beginning

* Jog at a comfortable pace for about 45 metres (50 yards).
* Slow down and walk for about 90 metres (100 yards).
* Repeat this cycle for a maximum of 20 minutes.

Aim to

* Gradually increase the distance you jog and reduce the distance you walk until you can jog comfortably for the entire 20 minutes. This means that you should be able to carry on a conversation while you jog.
* Very gradually increase your jogging to 30 minutes.

Starting young

Encourage your children to be physically active. Even young babies benefit from gentle exercise, and as they grow, regular physical activity will help them develop strong, efficient bodies and good coordination. Make the effort to take your children to the park or playground, where they can play tag with other children, run races and play on the climbing frame. Walking along the tops of low walls or the edge of the pavement with you there to steady them helps young children to develop their sense of balance. This, in turn, makes it easy for them to learn to ride a bicycle, which provides them with excellent exercise as well as a means of transport. Make sure their activities are safe, but don't be overprotective; encourage their sense of adventure and independence.

Join in your children's games, making them a family affair whenever possible. Most sports are suitable for the whole family too. You all will benefit from the exercise, of course, and as well as setting a good example for your children, you will have the opportunity to teach them about fair play and good sportsmanship. The whole family might also enjoy spending weekends or holidays fell-walking, rock climbing or skiing.

Remember that sports and games should be fun. Help your children to realize their full potential, but don't stress competition at the expense of enjoyment.

Helping you slim

Exercise is one of the most valuable slimming aids. When you exercise strenuously, your body responds with a small increase in the basal metabolic rate (BMR) – the rate at which it burns food energy. If you exercise regularly, the body gradually adjusts itself to maintain this higher rate all the time, using more energy even on days when you don't exercise. However, if you stop taking regular exercise, your BMR will slow down.

If you are following a healthy slimming diet and exercising regularly, you will begin to lose fat. At the same time, the exercise strengthens and tones your muscles. Muscle weighs more than fat, so although you may not notice a big drop in your weight, you will see a big improvement in your figure.

Index